THE
LAST MAN
STANDING

ALAN R. WARREN

WILDBLUE
PRESS

WildBluePress.com

THE LAST MAN STANDING published by:
WILDBLUE PRESS
P.O. Box 102440
Denver, Colorado 80250

ISBN 978-1-947290-89-1   Trade Paperback
ISBN 978-1-947290-88-4   eBook

Book cover design by Aeternum Designs
aeternumdesigns.com/
Interior Formatting/Book Cover Design by Elijah Toten
www.totencreative.com

THE
LAST MAN
STANDING

TABLE OF CONTENTS

A Question Of Guilt   5
From The Author   7
Preface   9
Prologue   12
Acknowledgments   16

Chapter 1 — Inmate #M33566   19
Chapter 2 — Out Of Time   38
Chapter 3 — Jack Mccullough's Prepared
                 Speech At Sentencing   51
Chapter 4 — Return To Innocence   57
Chapter 5 — Don't Give Up   64
Chapter 6 — Seeing Is Believing   69
Chapter 7 — Just Believe In Destiny   74
Chapter 8 — Extra! Extra! Read All About It   77
Chapter 9 — Back To Good   85
Chapter 10 — Truth Be Told …   88
Chapter 11 — Opening A Can Of Worms   92
Chapter 12 — Interrogation   95
Chapter 13 — What A Wicked Game To Play   139
Chapter 14 — Rape Trial Of Jeanne Tessier   150
Chapter 15 — Richard Schmack, I Need A Hero   158
Chapter 16 — FBI Timeline Report   169

Epilogue   185
About The Author   189
Sources   191

A QUESTION OF GUILT

Forward by Aphrodite Jones

After sifting through thousands of court documents, after conducting fascinating conversations with Jack McCollough himself, author Alan Warren proves just how difficult it is for a wrongfully convicted American to get justice.

When Jack McCollough was convicted of kidnapping and murdering 7-year-old Maria Ridulph in 2012, there were cheers from the gallery of a criminal courtroom in Illinois. This case had gone unsolved for five decades and at the time of his conviction, prosecutors boasted that they'd solved the coldest murder case in the nation's history.

This books takes us on a journey with Jack as he spends endless nights being violated and threatened by fellow inmates. It takes us back to 1957, on the snowy night when little Maria Ridulph disappeared in Sycamore, Illinois, and covers the subsequent investigation after Maria's body was discovered in April of 1958. Back then, dozens of FBI agents arrived to the town of Sycamore and interviewed hundreds of people, among them, Jack McCollough. The case became so high profile that at the time, both President Dwight Eisenhower and J. Edgar Hoover had taken an interest in it.

A break came in the case came 50 years after the crime, when in 2008, a call for the public to come forward with any information about Maria Ridulph's murder was announced. It was one of Jack McCollough's sisters, Janet Tessier, who emailed the Illinois State Police tip line, telling law enforcement that their mother, on her deathbed, claimed that her son, John Tessier (who later changed his name to Jack McCullough) was Maria Ridulph's killer.

That was the answer they'd been waiting for -- and Illinois police shifted into high gear. One of their first calls was to Kathy Chapmen, Maria's childhood friend who'd last been seen with the seven-year-old. Chapman was brought into police headquarters and was shown a line-up of six men. Though it had been five decades since Maria's death, Chapman pointed to Jack McCullough as the culprit.

In 2012, McCullough was convicted of Maria's murder. But was he guilty as charged? A few weeks after his conviction, a new State Attorney, Richard Schmack, was elected who had his own doubts about how the prosecution was handled. Working with attorneys from The Exoneration Project, Schmack looked into the case, scouring thousands of pages of evidence, including seeking missing evidence.

What he discovered about the conduct of the prosecution team and the police was shocking. He was persuaded that they'd convicted the wrong man.

In the end, McCollough's conviction was overturned, his name was cleared, and the finding of his innocence would allow him to qualify for compensation from the State of Illinois.

This book proves that (while, yes, the American justice system is still one of the best in the world) it is also a system that can be guilty of setting people up for a murder conviction.

It also leaves us wondering about the "best efforts" of law enforcement and about how many people have gotten away with murder and are still out there among us? Unfortunately, in the murder of Maria Ridulph, the case has been put back on ice, back into the cold case pile.

In this riveting account of guilt versus innocence, the author begs the question: how many other innocent people are currently serving time for crimes they didn't commit?

FROM THE AUTHOR

When I took on this book project, it started out similar to every book I had written before: find all of the court and police records and contact everyone who was still alive who had been involved in the crime. Throughout the writing from time to time, something deep inside was there that shouldn't have been. When I first met Jack McCullough, the road I was on reporting on this story changed quickly. During our conversation, Jack told me that the most important thing to get across to people was that what happened to him could happen to anybody. It was also very important to Jack that it not bring up any "dirt," and the focus remain on how he lost his freedom and how it could happen to anybody who read his story. That nobody was safe.

It took me about two years to actually know what Jack was referring to about keeping the dirt out of the story. You see, it was about that feeling deep inside, of Jack and all his family who became involved in this story. Something happened to create the catalyst that threw Jack out of his day-to-day life and into prison (which would make most people I know very angry), and I knew it would be the main focus in a book talking about Jack's life. But he wouldn't have it. This was what created a great conflict in me. On the top of it, I was going to tell the truth—the story and everything that people needed to know—or so I thought. But the feeling that something wasn't right worked its way out every time I wrote another chapter.

I have rewritten this book several times, and I just couldn't get it right. Until now. There's a part of the story that needs to be told, and though Jack doesn't want it in the book, I need to let the readers know. Not because of the salacious nature, but because it's the primary reason there *is* a story. So, I will only discuss Jack's sister where it's necessary only, as I need the readers to know that it's not because of embarrassment or shame, it's because he didn't want it to be the focus.

In the spring of 2012, Jeanne Tessier, half-sister to Jack McCullough, testified in court that Jack and two of his friends sexually assaulted her back in 1962 after giving her a ride in his new convertible car. Jack was charged with rape in DeKalb County for the alleged incident. Jack was acquitted after the two-day bench trial by Judge Robbin Stuckert, who said the prosecution failed to meet its burden of proof. McCullough showed no emotion during the trial, but cried afterwards when he was out of the public eye.

I originally thought that the false rape charge brought on by Jack's half-sister would have been a sore spot and something that would have created an anger that would drive Jack to going after her, using every opportunity he had to return the hurt she had given him through the course of the trial. But over the past two years, Jack not only never even suggested such a thing, but also never said a bad word about Jeanne.

I didn't know and had never met Jeanne, but learning about her life some, I will only say that I now believe the allegations that she made against Jack were false. She led a life of hurt and probably had great pain, and had made the same allegations on other occasions against other men. I only hope now that she found the peace that she probably searched for her whole life.

Jeanne Tessier died of breast cancer on January 10, 2018, in Louisville. She was 70 years old.

PREFACE

Every day, I leave my house to go to work, like all of you. On my drive, I always find myself drawn to a telephone pole that boasts a poster on it. I'm not sure why; the poster appears to be nothing special. In fact, it looks very old and faded. So much so, there is no way I could see anything that was on this poster. Perhaps it's the fact that I don't know what is written on this poster that keeps me fascinated?

It's the same every day, whether I'm totally engrossed in listening to "The Howard Stern Show" on Sirius XM or grooving to a great song. As I approach the location where the poster is, my mind goes straight to that poster and the thought of what could possibly be on it.

Finally, one day when it was not busy on the road and I had left early enough to have the time to stop at the telephone pole with the faded poster on it, I did. As I walked closer to it, I saw what looked like several dead flowers piled in front of the pole. They looked like they had been there for a long time. Long enough that the flowers were just dried up stems.

I looked at the poster, trying to see what had been on it. The years of rain and weather had torn, devoured, and faded most of the picture and writing, but on the lower left side, you could see that it had been a tribute to a young boy who had been killed somewhere close to this location, probably by a car; perhaps a drunk driver?

After reviewing the area as best as I could, I got back into my car and headed for work. I started thinking about how the events that led up to this tribute poster had happened. The young man must have been on the side of the road, perhaps riding his bike home from school, when a car recklessly drove by him, hitting and killing him. The details of this story couldn't be known unless I researched back through newspaper articles to try and find out about the death.

By this time, you are probably wondering why I'm putting these thoughts into the book. The whole two plus years that I have spent on this case, I have compared all the events in my life to that of this case. You see, every detail involved in our day-to-day life is important. Jack had lost his freedom and could no longer live in the freedom that we all do.

In the event of this youth who had been killed, the poster and dead flowers laying in front of the pole were what was left of his memory of being alive. Somewhere over the time since his death, his memory, which had been still alive in the family and/or friends who placed this poster and came to it to place flowers, was now gone. Whether they had died or simply moved on to continue living their own lives, I don't know. But it was that simple, and surely the same could be said about Jack.

From the time Jack stood in front of the judge to be pronounced guilty and taken into custody to now, the memory of his life has been slowly dissipating to nothing. As the people who surrounded the murder of Maria Ridulph in 1957 to now had all died, the frenzy created by the newspapers and TV at the time had moved on to the new stories of the day, the few distant survivors had started over in their new lives without Maria, and Jack was to sit silently in prison.

When we have nobody left on our side to remember what really happened and there is nothing left but faded pictures and memories, who is left but the last man standing, Jack Daniel McCullough?

At the end of my writing this book...

Finally, at the close of this book and after sending it to my publisher, I found myself returning to my home and driving on the same road as I have so many times before. Knowing that I have mentioned it in this book early on, I had great anticipation of seeing the poster of the boy who had lost his life when he was still so young. The wide range of emotions I felt throughout the process of getting Jack's story on to pages had made me extra sensitive to everything around me, and I had found myself buying some fresh flowers to leave at the telephone pole that bore the poster of the youth's life.

This time as I approached the site, I could see something was different. It was enough of a change that it had attracted my eyes immediately and was so strong I couldn't look away. The poster was gone. I could feel my heart pounding fast now and started to panic. Where had the poster gone? What happened?

As I pulled over at the pole, I got out and walked to the place where the old flowers had been left before. Everything had been cleaned up, cleared away. Was it that easy to walk away, and nobody was left to keep the memory alive? I slowly walked back to my car and sat in the front seat, staring ahead of me and not seeing anything.

After about five very long minutes, I took the flowers I had purchased earlier out of my car and walked toward the pole, where I placed them down on the ground in front of where the boy's picture used to be. It was then that I knew what Jack meant when he said "no dirt." I'm not sure what it was that he felt in his heart, but it certainly wasn't hatred; the people and the places that had caused such pain and difficulty in his life he had forgiven, and he just wanted to live with whatever he had left in his life.

PROLOGUE

At the time of Jack McCullough's 2012 trial and conviction, the case was subject to several news documentaries, including an episode of "48 Hours" on CBS, CNN, as well as a book written by Charles Lachman called "Footsteps in the Snow" in 2014, which became the basis of a Lifetime Movie Network documentary of the same name. This is where I became involved in this case, as I am one of the hosts of the popular true crime radio show called "House of Mystery," heard on KKNW 1150 AM in Seattle, and our guest was the author, Charles Lachman.

A portion of the proceeds of Lachman's book was being donated to the Maria Ridulph Memorial Fund, which was originally used to pay for a memorial map and later used as a scholarship, compassion, and summer camp fund for local children in need.

These works had been published before Jack McCullough's conviction was vacated, so they all presumed that the case had been successfully solved. So, when I interviewed Lachman, I found him to be very confident that McCullough not only kidnapped and murdered Maria Ridulph, but that he had also raped his half-sister, Jeanne Tessier, as well.

But throughout the interview, I found myself unconvinced of Jack's guilt. Lachman had presented no solid evidence— nothing physical, no DNA or witnesses. How could this man have been convicted of the kidnapping and murder of a 7-year-old who had gone missing back in 1957 with no real evidence?

I finished the interview thinking it was crazy not only to have a book on the murder but also a movie that totally dramatized the story and left the viewer with absolutely no doubt that Jack McCullough was guilty. It had, however, left me with way too much doubt.

It was about a month after the interview aired that I received a message on my Facebook account from a man named Casey Porter. I didn't recognize the name, but opened the message anyway. He told me that he was Jack McCullough's son-in-law, had heard the interview I did with Charles Lachman and really liked it, as I hadn't just presumed Jack did it with the evidence that Lachman had presented. He then told me more of the story, and that is where it all began.

Within two years, Jack McCullough's convictions of murder and abduction were vacated and he became a free man again. He returned to the Seattle area, where he had lived at the time of his arrest.

After Jack's release from prison, the first thing I thought was that somebody needed to tell the true story behind this case, what had happened behind the scenes, and what I meant were the facts. Not the feeling or emotions, but the facts. I knew then that I was the man to do the job, being a "just the facts" kind of writer. When I approached the publisher, the first response I got was "the story has already been done, there's even a movie about Jack!" My answer was quick. "Those books, the movie, and the TV news reports were all written on the basis that Jack was guilty, and that makes them wrong. There needs to be one that tells the truth. The real story." I also need to mention that I know for a fact the previous author, Charles Lachman, as well as the news programs that did shows on Jack from before the convictions were overturned, will not amend their stories and write a new edition to set the record straight. The true, full story from beginning to end.

Why authors like Charles Lachman won't amend their story, even when there is now sufficient evidence that has come out about the case, is an unknown. From Jack's side, you hear about the corruption and wrongdoings of law enforcement who handled this case (which we will discuss later on in this book), and Lachman just gets lumped in with that group.

My thoughts are that people like Lachman have pride in their work, and therefore quite often do not want to admit or change their work as it might cause some credibility issues in the future when they go to release a new book on another crime. It reminds me of some of the talk I heard about Jack's case that perhaps the police really believed that Jack was guilty, and therefore not only looked for evidence to help convict him but also fudged the evidence to make it work (we cover this theory and why it's not likely later on in this book as well).

No, it was by the end of researching and interviewing for this book that I came to the conclusion that it was simple pride in Lachman's case. It brings to mind when I needed to go in for my annual eye exam just a few weeks back. Everything went as it usually did, and for the most part, my prescription lenses stayed the same. So, when I went to the front desk afterwards and they asked if I wanted to pick new frames or keep the old ones, I decided to keep the old ones. After all, they were only a year old and I had never worn them once since I had bought them. You see, I do this every year; get a new updated pair of glasses for my eyes and as soon as I get home with them, I put them on my desk in front of my computer where I write so that I won't have to look for them when I need them. The only thing is, I never need them (or so I think). But each year that goes by, I can remember times where I have read something wrong. I read the item wrong because I couldn't see it correctly. It seems that each year I have more of these incidents, but I still don't wear my glasses. Why?

Of course, it keeps happening until I finally get told by a friend or somebody that I really need to start wearing my glasses or my eyes will just get worse. Why is it that we do things to ourselves that make life a little bit harder? It makes total sense to wear what my eyes need, but I don't. I know I'm not the only one who does this kind of thing, and we all do it with various things in our lives.

It's about our pride and our beliefs. If in our heart we really truly think something is true, no matter what we hear, we just won't accept anything else. Everyone has different levels of this behavior, from slight to extreme, such as all the conspiracy groups that have come alive as of late, like the Flat Earthers and the people who believe that we've never really been to the moon.

ACKNOWLEDGMENTS

JACK MCCULLOUGH

There is no possible way to know what Jack knows or feel what Jack feels, as I've never walked in his shoes. The life he has lived could not be captured in one simple book or movie. A person's life is so much more than what could ever be written.

We are all under the same sky, which gives us so many weather patterns. Such are our lives. It is only with great respect for Jack and the life that he has lived and shared with all of us, and only to make our lives better for knowing him and his story, that I could write this book.

CASEY PORTER

It is with profound respect and appreciation that I can write this book, as not only Jack's family, including his stepdaughter, Janey, and her husband, Casey Porter, but Jack, his attorney, and the few friends he has left, were all very open in communicating the truth, both positive and negative, of all the events as they happened. I could have never written such a book without them.

Remember, this story is about exposing the truth, corruption, and many problems with the current justice system in the United States of America. It is with great hope that all who read this book not only recognize the severe injustice that happened to Jack McCullough and his family, but also realize that these events could happen to any one of you reading this.

When I first met Jack, this message was the first thing that he told me. He repeated this statement many times through the hours that I spent with him. Jack also finished with this statement: "The most important thing to me in this book will be that people see the corruption for what it is, and that this story must be about that what happened to me could happen to anybody."

I must thank Casey, Jack's son-in-law, for the complete access to all the trial transcripts as well as the appeals and the current lawsuits, primarily against the Seattle Police Department as well as the Illinois State Police and the Sycamore Police Department.

DR. MICHAEL SHERMER

During the writing of this book, I have been heavily influenced by Dr. Michael Shermer, whom I hardly know as I have only interviewed him a couple of times over the phone when he was promoting two different books he had released over the past couple of years, "Heavens on Earth" and "The Moral Arc."

At my age now, I usually get the audio books, as my sight is not what it used to be and reading has become quite a strain. The books were read by Michael Shermer himself, which creates a much better audiobook, as the author reads it from their heart and you can feel what's important to him. It was perfect timing for me to have come across these books while I was writing this book. You see, Shermer writes from a scientific point of view about life, death, and God.

It was very poignant as I struggled with the case of Jack Daniel McCullough. It was a battle of morals in the areas of lies, blame, jealousy, hate, and even love, and all at the same time. So, with every day, I would find myself discovering something new during the writing that created an unrest in me. When I went to bed, it was time to listen to Shermer and see what he had to say about life. As I closed my eyes, an image of me lying on a shrink's couch would come into my head.

It was amazing how many times what Shermer was saying applied directly to what I had written earlier that day. That is, of course, except when he said things just happen by chance, that none of it was planned or meant to be!

By the end of it all, I came to realize that Michael's books were part of what gave me the strength to write this book—not by how the subjects related to my story, but to myself.

MY RADIO FAMILY

A special thank you to my Pop Family, who are all the things that exist around me. People who love me, hate me, or just feel indifferent to me, it is because of you that I'm able to write the way I do. You make me feel good, bad, loved, and hated. Thank you!

CHAPTER 1 — INMATE #M33566

I love meeting new people. I think everyone has a story to tell. We should all listen sometimes. – Kim Smith

I am reminded every day by things around me of just how easy it is to be fooled by appearances. This came to mind the first time I met Jack McCullough. In my mind, I was about to meet a man who was convicted of kidnapping and murdering a 7-year-old girl by the name of Maria Ridulph back in 1957 in Sycamore, Illinois.

After all, what could a man like this be like? What perception of that kind of man would you have if you knew nothing about him other than the reason he was convicted and put into prison? With this alone, I would think of a rough, heartless, maybe even sociopathic character.

After reviewing the interrogation tapes of Jack during the investigation of Maria's murder and finding as many pictures as I could, I thought that I was ready. I saw Jack as a large, mechanic-like figure, not easily swayed, and one who had no problem looking the detectives directly in their eyes during the questioning. He was obviously a smart man and knew how to talk with most anybody. Remember, this was before prison, so add a lot more aggression and anger along with the strength to survive prison with murderers, rapists, and men with absolutely nothing to lose as they were incarcerated for life.

Jack Mccullough in prison

It was a bright spring day in 2017 when I headed to the place I would meet with Jack. It was at a restaurant located in Edmonds, Washington, on the bay looking out on Puget Sound. It had a beautiful view of the Olympic Mountains and sandy beaches, with quite a few families out enjoying one of the first warm days in the Northwest.

When I arrived and parked, I started running through many of the questions that I wanted to ask Jack, trying to make sure that they sounded polite and respectful, but still invasive enough to explain the events in a logical way.

I looked out of my car window and noticed the back of a man's head wearing a cowboy hat. This was how I was to recognize Jack. I couldn't see his face, only his back, as he walked through the restaurant door and up the stairs to the dining room.

I quickly got out of my car, entered the restaurant, and ran up the stairs, not wanting to keep Jack waiting. As I reached the top step, I looked around the host area and noticed a gray-haired man with a cowboy hat standing patiently. He seemed small, much smaller than I expected. Could this be Jack?

I walked across the lobby to him, introduced myself, and asked if he was Jack. He smiled, said yes, and quickly excused himself as he had to use the washroom. When he got out, we were seated at a table that had an incredible view of Puget Sound. It was just then that a large man came up behind us, and Jack looked at him and said, "Hi, yes, this is okay. I'm okay with him, this is going to be fine."

I didn't realize that there would be someone else there, and why would there be?

Jack looked at me and said, "Yeah, he's just there to make sure that I'm okay, no problem." The first thing I asked Jack was if he got a lot of threats or had problems with people. "Oh, sometimes. There's still a lot of people that think I did it, you know? Even after they proved I didn't and let me go. I know how to read people; that's something I learned to do."

Jack then had a large smile as the waitress approached our table to take our drink orders. He was very polite and seemed really happy to be out having lunch. "I love it here," he said as he looked out over the bay. "When I first came here, I saw the ocean and knew I'd live here. I mean, who wouldn't fall in love?"

Just then, Casey Porter, Jack's son-in-law, came and sat down beside me. Jack asked Casey if he wanted lunch, but Casey said he just wanted to say hi and he had to go to work. "Well, okay," Jack responded, and then looked at me and said, "I couldn't make it without him. He's been great," referring to Casey, "but he thinks I'm a racist. Have you seen my book?" Jack asked me. I replied I hadn't. "Here," he said as he handed me a small, 60-page self-published book called "You Don't Know Jack." He explained that it was his memoir from his time in prison. Jack had kept a diary of sorts and after he got out of prison he decided to self-publish it. I was excited to read it, as it would give me a window into his thoughts during the time he had been incarcerated.

After Jack handed me the book, Casey got up and smiled, said his goodbyes to both of us, and left for his work. Jack stood up and shook his hand, and then returned to his seat and continued on about how Casey thought he was racist because of his book.

Jack's book has a section that talks about American society and how it tore apart the family by allowing women to work rather than stay home and care for the family. I could understand why people could jump to the judgment of it being misogynistic, but after taking a closer look at what Jack wrote and talking with him, I understand what it is that he was trying to get across to people.

Jack has a good memory of life with his mother running the household—not just cooking dinners, washing the clothes, and cleaning the house, but actually taking the time to care for the members of the household, solving their problems, and discussing events in life and their problems at school. Looking back, I think it was more about having someone to guide the children in their early life, and I can agree that it's more helpful to have that than not.

I'm not exactly sure why Jack brought that particular subject up. Maybe to try and clear the way or maybe to see how I felt about that kind of subject. Either way, I moved right on and asked him how his relationship with his mother was. Jack started to tell me how much he loved his mother before the waitress approached the table with our drinks and took our lunch order.

Jack, who was holding a copy of his book, then asked the waitress if she would like a copy. The waitress smiled and you could tell she was surprised, but she took it from him anyways. Jack is a very charismatic talker and always holds a smile, and it's a real smile. He is very genuine and really appears to love talking with people. He was so excited that the waitress was really interested in his book and story. Jack's expression reminded me of a man who just watched his favorite sports team win the big game.

As soon as the waitress walked away, Jack started to tell me about his life in England with his mother, and how during the war she met the man who would soon become his stepfather, and they moved to Sycamore, Illinois, in America to start a new life.

Jack would then proudly tell me about how while he was in prison he had learned four other languages. Not only did he learn to speak them, but he also learned to write them. Jack would jump around from subject to subject in his conversation. It almost seemed like he had so much to tell me, but not enough time to tell it.

Jack learned some of the toughest languages around, such as Chinese, Japanese, and Arabic, especially at an adult age. He told me that there were some really smart people in prison he had met who constantly worked on improving their minds. Jack would spend as much time as possible in the library trying to find out information about all sorts of things, including history. He told me that he had a lot of time to waste and wanted to put it to good use and learn something.

Jack told me he could have easily spent his time doing nothing or doing something useless, such as gambling. Jack then brought up how whenever somebody asked him when he would be getting out of prison, he would tell them that it would be the day he died. In his mind, he was never getting out of prison. This stuck in the back of my mind, and I wondered why a man who was sentenced to prison and thought he would never be getting out would spend so much time and effort on studying four languages and trying to gain so much knowledge about history?

The waitress brought our lunch to the table and after a quick exchange with her, we both began to eat. Jack had ordered a seafood pasta and I had a salad. I didn't say much while we were eating, and Jack mainly commented on the view while looking out the window at our table. You could see the love he had for the ocean and beach surroundings that Edmonds offered. It was the look of having seen the eyes of a long-lost love on his face.

It was after the waitress had cleared away our finished plates that Jack first looked me directly in the eyes with a more serious demeanor and told me that he didn't want any dirt in the story. He told me the minute I asked anything about sex, he would stop talking to me. I was taken aback for a second, but I really didn't have that thought in my mind, so I assured him that was not what I wanted in the story either. He finished by telling me not to ask about his sister.

After all of the pain and struggle Jack had been through in the last years, he was still protecting his sister. I found this to be admirable, and I think it also shows the kind of character that Jack possessed, even after his sister betrayed him. Jack then told me that as long as I told the truth and didn't print any dirt, I wouldn't have a problem with him.

"Did you know Maria Ridulph?" I asked directly.

"I only remember her when she was about 3 years old. Maria was walking down the street one day, as I was going to the store. This was only about 50 yards from her house, but very near a very busy street, where my dog got killed." Thinking about his dog being killed by a car, he decided to warn Maria. He told her she shouldn't be there, and to go home. Jack said Maria turned around and headed toward her home, and that was the last time that he saw Maria.

Jack described Maria as "so lovely," dressed like she was going to church. Jack had used that description before in other interviews he had done, and it created some back talk because of his use of the term "lovely." Jack would answer that by saying that it wasn't the correct term, that Maria was precious, and that all children that age were precious. We also have to remember that Jack was only a young teenager at the time that he reports this event happened with Maria.

Jack then went on, saying, "I'm a protector. I'm a born protector. I'm from a long line of military people."

Jack then started telling me about the corruption and injustice, and that the most important thing I could know was that what had happened to him could happen to anybody. Anybody could be convicted and sent to prison, even if they were innocent. Jack then went into his conviction and how the whole courtroom let out a loud cheer, and everybody was hugging each other, smiling, and even laughing.

Jack's first thought was that this was real; he was a convicted child killer. Jack was also a former police officer, and those were the biggest two things you did not want to be in prison.

After the conviction, they removed Jack from the courthouse under heavy guard and took him to jail. One of the most important things to Jack was to contact his wife once he got there to make sure she knew that he was okay. But the guards withheld Jack's code so that he was unable to call anybody, which left his wife to think that he didn't want to talk with her. Jack brought up the point that his wife had not been found guilty of anything, so why did they treat her so badly? It would be two months before Jack was finally able to call her.

Jack then told me how he had chosen well when he married her, as she stuck by him the whole time.

Eventually, Jack was taken to the maximum-security prison at Menard in Southern Illinois. Menard Correctional Center was officially opened in 1878 and was originally used as a military prison during the civil war. This was also the prison where executions were held by the state.

Jack told me that after you arrive at the prison, the guards make you get naked. They tell you to move your private parts, bend over, spread your cheeks, and cough. After your shower, they give you your clothing and bedding. He then told me that the cells were like dungeons, very cold and damp, and most times you would sleep with your clothes on to keep warm.

The first three months Jack was in Menard, he said there were three inmates who were killed as well as a pastor and two guards who were beaten badly in the church.

Jack then went on to talk about his experience when he arrived at Pontiac Correctional Center in Illinois. Because of Jack's heart condition and age, they gave him the bottom bunk in his cell. The bottom bunk in prison is always given to the toughest or meanest guy, and that just happened to be the guy who lost his bottom bunk to Jack! The guy was a Texan mechanic who had murdered somebody, and when he returned to his cell to find Jack was in his bed, he was livid. To top things off, he found out that Jack was an ex-cop and child kidnapper and murderer; all the more reason to kill him. It would not even take two days for the Texan to threaten to slaughter Jack. Jack reported it to the guards, and soon after he was moved to another cell with a different cellmate. Jack said that the new cellmate was short and he didn't consider him much of a threat, which he later found out was a mistake.

The day after he had been placed in his new cell, Jack took his afternoon shower and went back to his cell to take a nap. Shortly after he fell asleep, he thought he was dreaming and something kept hitting his head. Before opening his eyes, Jack brushed his face with his hands to try and stop the feeling of whatever was hitting him. He then felt something long and pen-shaped slip through his fingers. He opened his eyes quickly and saw his cellmate viciously stabbing at his face with what appeared to be a toothbrush.

The toothbrush penetrated through to the back of Jack's eye socket twice. His eye filled with blood and popped out of the socket by about half an inch. Jack quickly sat up and pushed his eye back into the socket, which forced a large squirt of blood to fly out about six feet. The cellmate attempted to keep on stabbing Jack with his toothbrush, but now he was only able to reach Jack's back and the side of his head and was able to cut Jack's ear. Soon, the guards came, stopped the attack and eventually took Jack to the hospital, where the doctors were able to help Jack regain his eyesight.

Jack then told me how corrupt things were, and his message was to tell people to do something about it before they, too, became a victim like he was.

"These folks tried to destroy me; they found people to lie about me," Jack firmly stated. "They have manufactured evidence and gave false testimony to the grand jury," he continued. "They all profited and enjoyed some fame, and some have retired with good retirement. Some still have their jobs, so we are all in danger from these corrupt officials who neither know nor care about the Constitution. This story is bigger than me; it's about what they can do to you."

The waitress brought over the bill for lunch and Jack refused to let me pay. He grabbed it and paid for lunch. He stood up and suggested we go to a park down the road and talk more. I agreed and followed Jack into the parking lot. He turned around and asked if I wanted to ride with him. I declined. I didn't want to leave my car in the parking lot, as it was a foreign car I had driven down from Canada and I didn't feel comfortable leaving it alone there. Jack smiled and said that he knew I wouldn't, because I didn't trust him, and he laughed. "You see? I do know how to read people."

We both got into our cars and I followed Jack to a park that was located only a few miles away from the restaurant. We parked. Jack walked to a picnic table located up on a hill in the park that overlooked the beach and Puget Sound and sat down. I followed him over to the table and sat across from him. He looked up and asked me what I wanted to know.

For some reason, I was at a loss for what to ask. I was still thinking about how I could find out more about Jack's relationship with his sisters. I wanted to know why his sister would lie about Jack in the way she did. I was still thinking about the family dynamic and trying to figure out what could have happened in the past between the family members. Now, I look back at my train of thought, see how wrong it was and what the real story was surrounding the events that happened to Jack, exposing the reasons it happened and that it wasn't really about his family relationships. After all, the injustice that happened to Jack could happen to anybody; it wasn't about the breakdown in his family, but the breakdown in the justice system and the members behind the corruption who run the legal system now.

Quite often throughout the day, Jack would stop talking, or just after he'd ask a question, he would look me dead in the eyes, smile, and sing "O Canada." This was one of those moments. Even though he had done this several times already, it would make me stop thinking about the case and return his smile.

Jack then asked me if I had ever met Jeff Doty, the man who wrote the book about him called "Piggyback." I told Jack that I had interviewed Jeff, he seemed like a real nice guy, and that I had also interviewed Charles Lachman, the author of "Footsteps in the Snow," which was also turned into a Lifetime movie. He then sneered and told me that Lachman wouldn't know anything about the truth. I could tell that he was upset by Lachman because of his work on the story.

Lachman, to me, seemed like a nice guy both times I had interviewed him years earlier, but I do question his motives in not only writing his book the way he did, with Jack being guilty with absolutely no doubt, but also making a movie out of the script at a time when we all knew Jack was to be released from prison with his conviction overturned.

Not wanting to have the rest of the afternoon focused on Lachman and his work, I steered the discussion toward how he was treated by people now that he had been released from prison. He answered me by saying that people will believe what they want to, but he also didn't care. "I am not important, so they can say what they want. Most people were told lies about me, and the liars will be exposed, and that will make my time spent in prison count for something."

I thought that we had spent enough time together by now to follow up on the question of Jack being a racist at the very beginning of our meeting. I asked Jack why Casey considered him a racist; after all, thinking that the mother of a family should stay home to take care of the home rather than go out and work a job is hardly what I would consider racist.

Jack responded by telling me the story of when one of the judge's employees asked Jack what caused him stress, and Jack had answered, "Blacks, Muslims, and Democrats." Even though he was halfway joking with her, he blamed that slip of the lip on the fact that all of his cellmates fit at least one, and sometimes all three, of those labels.

From that conversation, Jack then went into how the climate was not changing, either, and there was no global warming, saying, "There's good weather and bad weather." Jack then asked, "Do you know what hurricanes and tornadoes are?" I stayed quiet and Jack answered the question himself. "Bad weather! That's all it is, just bad weather, and these liberals try to make it a big deal."

Jack then attacked the schools as liberal or socialist, saying they have dumbed down the people, which makes them easier to control. Jack was thrilled that the election had taken out so many liberals and the people were taking back their country.

It was then that I felt like I was listening to one of those conspiracy shows that have gained so much popularity lately, where everything that has gone wrong was actually engineered by a certain group of people. He continued, "You need to get rid of all liberals and socialists! The liberal union teachers try to make American children read from the Quran yet refuse to read the Lord's prayer."

At this point, I understood how the racist label could be applied toward Jack. But it must be said that in the same conversation with Jack, he would tell me about showing compassion to a very strong black man he was in prison with. The black prisoner had prostate cancer and had killed three people, which is what put him in prison. He had no family or support and didn't want to live anymore, so Jack would walk the track with him for hours to lift his thoughts from suicide.

Jack would tell me he would do such things because he wanted to find purpose wherever he was, even prison. "You have to make yourself valuable."

Jack strongly believes that we are all here for a purpose.

I had to ask Jack why he had learned so many languages and spent so much time on them while being in prison, as in Jack's own words, his end date in prison would be the day of his last breath. So, was it an act of a racist man to help another prisoner who he was in jail with, who was black, to feel better about his life and not to commit suicide? I'm not sure I can make the determination of what was in Jack's heart, especially in such a short time knowing him.

It was certainly obvious to me at this point that Jack was a much more complex person than I expected, as were the subjects of race and the politics of people. I do know that when Jack would talk about these subjects, there was a distance in his eyes, and just at the moment where he would come back to where he was in the now, he would stumble and probably wonder if he had said too much and what would come back to him.

Jack didn't need to worry about that with me, as I knew that his goal wasn't to prove his politics or his racist beliefs or anything, even about his guilt on the murder case. He knew he was innocent. He knew that no matter how or what people thought about him, it didn't matter or make any difference. The only thing he wanted to do was to warn people, warn everybody who would listen, that what had happened to him could and would most definitely happen to anyone, and that you had to be prepared.

So, the last thing that he wanted us to focus on was his feeling about society in America and what was causing the problems in the country.

"So, Jack, why learn so many languages and culture while in prison?"

Jack went back to the time when he was an intelligence analyst in the Vietnam War, where his target was Asia. It was during that time Jack had become very interested in the Japanese language. His interest then continued with Korean, Arabic, Chinese, ancient Egyptian, and even some of the dead languages.

The Vietnam War seemed to have had the most impact on how Jack was living today. He said it took him 10 years to get over the war, and only about four to get over prison. Perhaps he felt more in control of his reactions during and after prison, whereas because the war was his first major experience with death and killing all around him, it had more of an impact?

Jack told me that "something as simple as a traffic ticket can turn into a warrant. People can lose their job, then their car, and even their apartment from a simple crime just because they don't have the money to buy themselves the protection they need. I was convicted on a lie by an incompetent judge who happened to be trying his first murder case. He was a traffic court judge beforehand."

It was this same judge who would not allow the FBI reports of Jack's case into the trial, as he ruled them hearsay. That would be the key to the conviction. Jack referred to that as a setup, a conspiracy just to convict a man they knew was innocent. It was the decision of the judge that because the body of Maria Ridulph was found in the state of Illinois, the FBI investigation would be sealed and not used as the crime only happened in one state. In this book, I have attached the whole FBI report timeline and shown why it would have not been possible for Jack to commit this crime, as well as the most likely suspect that the FBI had at the time. This man would later be convicted of molesting his own daughter and placed in prison, where he died.

Jack was staring at the kids playing in the park we sat in, and I said, "It's still a bit cold for the kids to be playing in the sand." Jack then started to explain about the two courtyards he had in the prison he was in.

"The yards were quite messy, muddy through the winter and hot and dusty places in the summer." The guard would yell out "Yard!" and everyone would line up according to the floor they were on and cell groups they were in. Jack's main goal was to walk when he got out into the yard, but that would attract who Jack called "the Predators."

Some religious guy might try to recruit you into their prayer group, and because Jack was considered to be a child rapist, he thought it would be better to make friends rather than have another guy in prison hate him or want to kill him.

As most of his time was spent in a cell, it was very important to use the time out in the yard to get his exercise. Jack would also begin to weight lift. He told me he had a lot of respect for the guys who belonged to the 300 club, whose name came from each member being able to bench press at least 300 pounds. "They got my respect because they were disciplined and took care of each other."

The world in prison was more primal and basic, where it was purely survival of the fittest. There were no protections for the weak or rules to try and equal out the playground for those without skills. It was the opposite direction from the world of freedom found in modern-day America. Perhaps this was more like the country used to be in older times, and more like what Jack would like to see come back to the country? Perhaps this is also why Jack has such harsh words for any minorities, liberals, or unions?

Jack then told me that he would like to limit the amount of time prisoners get sentenced to, and in fact regulate the amount of time that a judge can sentence to someone convicted of a crime.

As I started to wonder in more detail about the way the Jack would like to see the prisons run, his voice faded.

I can fully agree with Jack's sentiment of the justice system not being sound, but I don't see privatization as the one-answer solution. Throughout my life, I have never seen any large company, such as it would have to be in order to run a vast operation like a prison, perform any more of a competent job than the government has. This is not to say that the government is not corrupt and doesn't have its shortfalls, but it's the largest of companies in this country that create large environmental disasters such as the *Exxon Valdez* oil spill, the same as BP. It's the largest of companies that have held back providing a proper medical system for its employees, or even offer proper wage increases. Yes, as Jack said to me, it is businesses that know how to save money, not waste, but it is usually at the cost of the employees who work for them. It's not that they are more efficient in running the day-to-day operation; in truth it's actually that they cut on service and never supply good service. It is with those conditions that you want the prisons run?

I don't know personally what it's like to be incarcerated as I have never been in jail, but I'm not sure that you would have any more of a happy employee guarding the prison under a large corporation. Why would they be? They would not have anything more in either wage or support for doing their job.

It is very important to remember that we belong to the life and keep the hope. Hope is what keeps us alive in the dark cell when all we have is the sound of our souls.

Jack's voice slowly came back into my head while he was explaining the day-to-day life in the prison. "Did you know that there are certain rules that cellies have to follow—not from the prison, but between inmates?" I replied to him as quickly as I could, hoping he wouldn't notice I hadn't been paying attention to what he was saying.

"No. Why don't you tell me about them?"

"Well, the cells are only five feet wide, so when cellies need to pass each other, they do it back to back. This also makes it so that only one person has the floor to use the toilet or sink, leaving the other guy to his bed. In fact, if one guy was using the toilet, the other guy would stay in his bed, or if he was standing, he would be facing looking out through the bars."

Jack described that once in prison, the guards control every aspect of your lives from when you eat to when you exercise and even when you go to bed. You no longer have control over anything physical. You are left with only your mind, and it's what you do with your mind and thoughts that will make for how the rest of your life is going to be—not only for the time you have left in prison, but of the time after you've been released, if you are going to be released, into the world again.

Jack would walk around with a constant fear, as not only was he an ex-cop, but a convicted child killer as well. An attack could happen anywhere and at any time. He could be stabbed in the yard while walking; it was pretty common for inmates to have their makeshift knives hidden out on the grounds.

Jack would constantly be watching his back. Walking down a stairway, he would have a strong grip on the rail, as another inmate could push him down the flight of stairs. It would be during the commotion that he could get stabbed.

Even with cellmates who seemed to have bonded with Jack, he would have one eye open at night during sleep time, because as he told me, "If you get too comfortable with your cellie, you can end up dead."

There was a certain chill in the air now, and a slight wind started to blow. It was a quick reminder that it was still early in the springtime, and even though the sun was shining brightly, night was beginning to set in as the sun started to set.

Jack wanted to know if there was anything that he could help me with, and I told him that I felt I had enough for a great start and needed time to properly process what I had learned from him throughout the day.

Jack thanked me again and reminded me that he didn't want any dirt in the book, and as long as I wrote the truth, I wouldn't have any problems with him. I agreed and told him that there would be nothing but the truth, I would keep it as dirt-free as I possibly could, and that the focus of the book would be on his warning for others to be aware that what had happened to him could happen to anybody in the country.

It was on that comment that I thought I'd ask the question that might be the most sensitive to him. "Why do you think that your mother lied about your father picking you up and you being in the house that night?"

Jack quickly responded, "I have no idea and I wish she hadn't."

"Do you think that she was worried that you might be guilty?" I asked.

"She was frightened. After all, this was the FBI."

Driving back home, I thought to myself how nothing lasts forever, including lies told, and that in a matter of time we all will find our freedom. Was it Jack who somehow lost his way, or had the justice system? Perhaps it was, as Jack would say repeatedly, that everything and everyone has its purpose, and it's not really about a lost way, it's just about "a way."

I could feel that my hands were tired holding the steering wheel of my car while driving on the interstate. I couldn't help thinking that Jack was not interested in getting money from a lawsuit for his wrongful prosecution and the years that he had spent in prison. Even now, after his release, his mind was set on what he knew was truly important: his wife, or best friend as he called her. She was the one who stood by him through it all. He was focused on getting the word out about how the terror of being imprisoned wrongly as well as the corruption of the police and judge on his case could have their way with you, or anybody in the country. Jack was still set on directing the attention from his sister, who had lied and wrongly accused Jack, as Jack's character wouldn't permit him to attack her or let anyone else for that matter.

It is my opinion that this chapter is the most important chapter in this book, as it gives you insight into Jack from his own words. In the rest of part one of this book, I have covered the trial, which ended with Jack being convicted of the murder of Maria Ridulph. Also included are the FBI files, which Jack and his attorneys tried to have admitted into evidence but were rejected by the judge, who decided they were hearsay. As well, I have included the sentencing statement made by Jack.

Part two of this book will cover the story where this all began, back in 1957 in Sycamore, Illinois, and a 7-year-old innocent girl who was just focused on the first snowfall of the year and going out to play one night. It would be the last time she had the safety that she found every time she looked into her mother's eyes, or the security when she sat on her father's lap before bed.

CHAPTER 2 — OUT OF TIME

A single thought leaves a trace

It was Friday, September 14, 2012. The fifth and final day of the trial. It was a cool day in Chicago, with temperatures around 60 degrees, cloudy and foggy, and an umbrella was needed as it had been raining on and off all day. The weather was not the only reason you would feel the need to bundle up, as not only was it the day that the verdict of Jack McCullough was about to be announced, there was something much larger going on in the world scene that would soon take the attention away from all other stories for many years to come.

Earlier that week, protests generated by an American-made film called "Innocence of Muslims" that mocked the Prophet Muhammad continued to flare for a fourth day across the Middle East and North Africa. In Egypt, police in riot gear used tear gas against demonstrators who were hurling rocks at the U.S. Embassy. The Muslim Brotherhood canceled a "million men" protest scheduled to follow Friday prayers, but protesters continued to gather, and some reportedly moved to burn an American flag. In Yemen, protesters breached a security wall and set fire to a building inside the U.S. Embassy compound on Thursday. Four protesters died and dozens of people were injured as security forces clashed with demonstrators. Protests against the film had erupted in multiple other locations, including Bangladesh, Malaysia, Indonesia, Iraq, Iran, Jordan, Sudan, Tunisia, Israel, and the Gaza Strip. All of this led to the attack on the embassy in

Benghazi, with the killing of four Americans, including the ambassador to Libya, J. Christopher Stevens.

In the courtroom, everyone had gathered with anticipation of what the verdict would be. There was nervous chatter when they brought Jack into the courtroom. It was slightly after 11 a.m. as they returned from a recess. The evidence had all been completed, the closing arguments were done, and all the attorneys were present when the judge began to speak. There was electricity in the air.

There was a long pause. The air was stale with tension. Emotions were high and in total conflict. As you looked around the room, there was no feeling as to what was about to happen.

The judge folded closed the verdict paper and removed his glasses, placing them slowly onto the bench. He then scanned around the court, looking to see if there was anything unusual happening. All was clear.

He started by clearing his throat, almost a cough-sounding noise; perhaps the thought of what he was about to say was slowing him down on pronouncing the verdict.

"It is with much thought, care, and consideration that based on the totality of the evidence the court has heard over this week, the court finds that the defendant has been proven guilty." There was a loud outburst from the public gallery. There was cheering and clapping. It even sounded like there was laughter. Judge James Hallock slammed his gavel on the bench. *"You'll all be cleared out of here. I'm not finished. You'll all be cleared out of here if there's one more outburst!"*

"The court finds from the totality of the evidence the defendant has been proven guilty beyond a reasonable doubt for the three charges contained in the indictment. Now, at this point, we'll order a pre-sentence investigation and we'll need a court date in about eight weeks' time, and

I would suggest that we go to November 30 at 11 o'clock. Hopefully, there will be a courtroom available. Order to come."

The prosecutor, Mr. Escarcida, asked if he might speak.

Judge: *"Just a minute. Now—sit down. Now, sir, it's important for me to remind you that you have the right to an appeal. If you do file an appeal, you must file an appeal within 30 days. If you are unable to retain counsel, the court will appoint a free appellate counsel for you. The court will also see to it that if you are unable to afford it, you'll receive a free copy of the transcript from this week's trial. And did the state have one other request or comment?"*

Mr. Escarcida: *"Yes, Judge. The people now have a motion to revoke this defendant's bond."*

Judge: *"The defendant's bond will be revoked. He'll be held now without bond and I'll ask the clerk to go back to chambers to take all the evidence and for the clerk's office to maintain the evidence pursuant to their normal custom."*

The judge then got up from the bench and retired to his chambers, with the clerk following closely behind him.

Jack was still in shock and could hardly feel the guards as they placed his hands behind his back and started to cuff him. Even when they put the chains around his feet, he could feel nothing. He was so deep in thought and barely conscious. It was like dreaming, where you're so focused on what's happening around you in the dream that you can't feel anything physical.

Slowly, they walked Jack from the courtroom toward the door that leads defendants to the lock-up cell, where he was to wait to be taken to jail until sentencing later in November. Just then, he snapped out of the haze in his mind in time for his eyes to connect with Janey, his stepdaughter, and he mouthed the words "I love you."

It was now all going faster than the speed of light, and in the back of Jack's mind, he was trying to remember where this all began. It was at that point when Jack realized that his life was now about to change into something that he never saw coming.

We all feel like we are in control of our lives, deciding where we want to go and what job we want to have, but over time what we perceive as freedom might just be fantasy. Was this all just synchronicity? Carl Jung once wrote, "How are we to recognize causal combinations of events, since it is obviously impossible to examine all chance happenings for their causality? The answer to this is that causal events may be expected most readily where, on closer reflection, a causal connection appears to be inconceivable."

Were all of these events meant to happen, or was it the freedom of choice of all the people involved that led Maria to be killed and Jack to be convicted of the crime, albeit wrongfully?

SENTENCING

Sentencing happened on the morning of Monday, December 10, 2012. The chill outside in the near-freezing weather was nothing in comparison to the way it felt in the courtroom. After the court went through the formalities, the judge looked to the defense and asked, *"Does the defense have any evidence to present now?"*

Defense attorney: *"Judge, we have two statements. I'd like to read both into the record."*

Judge: *"Sure. We ask that the clerk be able to make copies as we appear to only have one here."*

Defense: *"The first is from the defendant's wife, and I'll tender the original to you when I'm done."*

The defense attorney then read the statement from Jack's wife, which read:

"I've been married to Jack for almost 19 years. I know what's in his heart and soul. I've seen him with our grandchildren. He's kind and loving to them and has never raised his voice to them. Jack couldn't and wouldn't harm a child. He isn't a violent man. The judge and the prosecutors were given the FBI files that are in the box that prove he wasn't in Sycamore when Maria was taken. The judge convicted him anyway. You have to ask yourself why he was convicted. Do the words 'beyond a shadow of doubt' sound familiar to anyone? There is no evidence to convict him except a woman in her 60s trying to remember someone she saw when she was 8 years old and hadn't seen in 55 years. Can any of you identify someone you haven't seen in 55 years? I think not. Any attorney will tell you that an eyewitness is very unreliable regarding a current crime. How about an eyewitness who was 8 years old at the time and is now trying to remember 55 years back?

"During the trial, a female prosecutor pointed to Jack and called him a coward. He is far from a coward. Jack served his country in the Army, and after years of hard work, he eventually became a captain, not behind a desk where it's safe, but on the ground, leading a group of frightened young men into battle.

"Jack was convicted beyond a shadow of a doubt by a judge from DUI court who received a promotion to a better court soon after convicting my husband. Two of the three prosecutors were fired. Clay Campbell lost the election. That's a little strange, since he never tired of telling the press how happy he was to bring closure to the family. That was going to be the key to getting elected, because Campbell solved the oldest cold case in U.S. history. How can Campbell bring closure to anyone when convicted the wrong man? The most troubling part is that everyone knew

he was not guilty, but convicted him anyway. Judge, you may be able to send him to prison for however many years he has left on this Earth, but I won't be silenced. Everyone will know about the corruption in DeKalb County.

My husband, Jack, was convicted just to close the oldest case in U.S. history. The fact that he was innocent didn't matter to anyone. Everyone who had a hand in convicting Jack all knew from the FBI files that he was innocent. You should all be ashamed of yourselves. Tell us, Judge, what is the punishment for an innocent man?"

The courtroom was stone cold silent, not a sound. The defense attorney turned around, facing Jack, and placed the letter on the table in front of him. For the first time, Jack looked up for a brief second and stared coldly at the judge. The judge then placed his glasses on and started to look at papers that were on his bench, as if to avoid Jack's eyes.

Janey 'O Conner (Jack's Step Daughter)

Defense: *"Secondly, from Janey O'Connor, and by the way, Judge, Janey O'Connor flew from Seattle here last time the matter was in court. Simply because of timing, she was in the air when we decided to continue the sentencing, so she did come here, she got to see her stepdad, but was unable to stay here and unable to return, so she leaves you with her written statement."*

Janey's statement reads as follows:

"My name is Janey O'Connor. I am Jack Daniel McCullough's stepdaughter. He is the man I call Dad. He is the man my children call Grandpa.

1. Jack came into my life and started dating my mother when I was 12 years old. When I was 14, Jack and my mother decided to get married. On the day he applied for a marriage license in April of 1994, he also changed his name from John Tessier to Jack McCullough in honor of the nickname my grandfather had given him and his mother's maiden name.

2. Growing up with Jack in my life was a challenge. Not a challenge for myself, but a challenge for Jack. I was not the easiest teenage girl to deal with, to say the least. Jack was a good father to me, always patient, always there for me no matter what I did or how I treated him. Jack loved me even during the times I did not deserve his love and trust. He never showed anger towards me, never made me feel uncomfortable. If I was ever in trouble of my doing or otherwise, Jack was the one that I called, and Jack was the rock that was always there for me.

3. In all my experience with Jack, all the time we were doing activities together, shooting, time around the house, walking the dogs, discussions on literature and politics, Jack never, and I emphasize never, touched me inappropriately or gave any inkling he would ever do anything sexually to me. The idea of Jack being inappropriate never crossed my mind.

4. Before my mother married Jack and when he still went by the name of John Tessier, Jack's sister, Jeanne Tessier, called my mother to tell her just what an evil man Jack was. I was on the other phone throughout the entire conversation, and although Jeanne went on and on about how abused she was, she never told my mother she was raped, but she did tell my mother she knew Jack wanted to hurt her because he told her she was pretty and by the way he looked at her. As a 14-year-old girl, I was very confused about the entire half-hour conversation, but what Jeanne has said in the last year is not close to what she told my mother in 1993 about the man I was to call Dad.

5. When Jack was arrested in June of 2011, I was shocked. I did not know what to believe after reading the arrest report. Things about a sweater, train tickets, abuse, et cetera. When Jack was first arrested, my only concerns were how the police had lost his glasses, making him blind and unable to read and sign important documents, how they had messed up his heart medication, sending him to the hospital a half a mile from the jail, how Jack had sat for a lie detector, yet all the police would ask was about the Milton case, how the man I called my dad had been stuck in a chair for six hours without his heart medication, without an attorney, with no consideration that he worked the graveyard shift and had been up for almost 24 hours straight, with everyone around him just pushing for him to admit to something, as it turned out they had no evidence he did.

6. It was mentioned that Jack's sister claims to have never seen the sweater after Maria went missing. This information was sensationalized and printed in many news sources. Never once was it mentioned that less than a week after Maria disappeared, Jack was on active duty. Of course, the sisters never saw the sweater again. Jack was not home to wear it. The train ticket that an ex-girlfriend happened to have in a framed photo of a boy she dated 55 years ago was another piece of evidence that was widely reported. After reading that in many articles, I went online and found on eBay an unused train ticket from 1957 for December 4 that was up for auction. I could find this in a matter of moments. If I had 55 years, I'm sure I could have found one for the exact date of the disappearance. I have many friends that hang on to such items such as train tickets from trips as mementos. The difference today is we live in a much different environment that 5 years ago. Security has very much changed in the last half a century. However, the thing that matters most is not how Jack got to Rockford, but what time the three military officers reported seeing him and what time made the collect phone call from Rockford to his family home requesting a ride home?

7.   When Jack was arrested, I did not know if he had committed the crime or not. The crime took place 20 years to the day before I was born. What Jack had or had not done nearly 20 years before I came into this world was something that would not take away the man he was to me and I wanted to be there for him as he was there for me all those years, no matter what the truth was. My heart told me he was innocent, but logically I knew it was possible for someone to portray one version of himself and keep another one hidden. In the month following Jack's arrest, I visited him at the jail, exchanged letters, and did a lot of reading about the case on my own. Jack did not know at the time the FBI had a report which made it plain that not only did he not commit the crime, but that he was in Rockford at the time. My dad felt the medical records from the Army would prove his innocence. It was amazing to all how the FBI records completely clear my father. The day I realized Clay Campbell had read the FBI reports before having my dad arrested was a very hard day for me. My faith in the judicial system is completely altered. Whether or not the FBI records are admissible in a court of law or not, no adult could read those records and still believe Jack, my dad, committed this crime. I believe in the United States we have the best judicial system. However, our system is only as good as the men and women in it. As good as our system is, it is still flawed. Our legal system is corrupted and manipulated by the egos, desires, and wants of the men and women who comprise it.

8.   Over the last year and a half, Jack has sent me dozens of thoughtful letters as well as letters and pictures to my children, who call him Grandpa. I have spent the last year and a half reading all the evidence in the case and reading all the reports contemporaneous to the years after the murder happened. I have tried to steel my emotions and be objective, and after reading everything, I do not see one shred, not one ounce of proof, that my dad committed this crime. Until Clay Campbell got involved in this case. Based on all the news articles, statements from Maria's mother, statements from Kathy Chapman, and all reports, the abduction happened at 7 p.m. At 7 p.m., my dad made a collect call from Rockford, as verified by the FBI. He could not have committed this crime. If there was proof that my father had committed this crime, I would still love him and stand beside him. I would want him to face the punishment that he deserved. I would support Jack because I know he would do the same for me. However, I would not be the one voice shouting his innocence. The prosecution should not benefit from waiting 55 years to prosecute a case. The only benefit of time should be advancement of technology, but that is not the case here. The state has benefited greatly in the passage of time. Three military officers are no longer able to testify and corroborate Jack's alibi. The FBI agents that investigated the case are no longer alive to validate the hard work they put into the investigation. Military records have been destroyed by a fire, and Jack's sister is allowed to speak for a woman who is no longer alive to speak for herself.

9. I do not believe Kathy Chapman is able to identify a man she spent just a few brief moments with 55 years ago. I do not believe that at eight years old she was able to identify the man last seen with Maria. I believe the reason she gave three different descriptions in the days following Maria's disappearance is due to the fact she was not able to identify or describe the man.

10. Two weeks after Maria was taken, Kathy traveled to Milwaukee to view a live lineup, and there, in the accompaniment of the FBI, she positively identified a man that not only could not have committed the crime but did not resemble my dad at all. Kathy testified she had no memory of identifying anyone other than my father. How is it that she is able to identify a man that she spent such a brief period of time with, yet is unable to remember such a major event in her life? I would not expect her to be able to 55 years later describe a man she identified or even describe the name of the FBI agents that were present. However, I would expect her to remember this major event in her life. For me, this calls into question her ability to recall memories. Did Kathy know that the defense would not be allowed to produce the FBI record that proved she made this identification or did she simply not remember such a major event in her life? I'm left wondering if perhaps her close personal relationship with Jack's sisters might have aided her recovery of the memory of the man last seen with Maria or even create the memory of the man she remembers from so long ago. I have read that Kathy and the Tessier sisters have been friends for many years. I wonder if the face she now remembers is just the face she saw in so many pictures in the Tessier family house. Maria's brother is quoted as saying, "The only thing I can come up with is those involved looked at Jack and only saw one lone old man." Perhaps they think sacrificing one innocent old man is worth giving an entire community a false sense of closure and a legal team notoriety. What they do not see is the family standing behind Jack. They do not see the loving wife who desperately wants her husband home, the grandchildren who miss their grandfather, the in-laws who have become Jack's family, and the daughter who desperately misses the strength and love that Jack provides.

11. The week after my dad was arrested, I was quoted in hundreds of news sources stating my dad was innocent. I am here today to tell you again, Dad is innocent. I hope the pain caused to my family is worth the five minutes of fame you all have received. This case is unprecedented, and in the future, I am positive it will be overturned on appeal. Those involved and the decisions made in this case will be scrutinized, and I can only hope the people involved will be held accountable for their actions. In the week after the abduction, my dad took a polygraph test administered by the FBI. I would like to see these people, some of whom are in this courtroom, take the same test relating to many things about this case. Again, my name is Janey O'Connor. Jack McCullough is my dad. Jack McCullough is innocent.

The judge responded by thanking the defense attorney and asking if there was any other evidence. The attorney replied that there was not. The judge then turned to the prosecution and asked if he had any evidence to submit. Mr. Escarcida, the prosecutor, responded that the state would like to present evidence in both aggravation and mitigation as well as sentencing recommendations.

"First of all, Judge, with respect to the charge of murder, the state is asking this court to sentence Jack Daniel McCullough to natural life in prison. For the offense of kidnapping, Your Honor, the state is asking for the maximum penalty per 1957 of five years in prison. With respect to the charge of abduction of an infant, Your Honor, the state respectfully asks this court sentence Jack Daniel McCullough to natural life in prison."

He then followed with a statement: *"Judge, Jack Daniel McCullough, or as he was previously known back in 1957, John Tessier, now stands convicted. He's been convicted of the murder of a little girl. He is a cold-blooded killer. He's had his day in court. Nothing about this trial was a sham. There was no conspiracy. This case was not about Clay Campbell. This was about one person, Jack McCullough, and his sick behavior, the crimes that he committed back in 1957, pure and simple."*

CHAPTER 3 — JACK MCCULLOUGH'S PREPARED SPEECH AT SENTENCING

"Keep love in your heart. A life without it is like a sunless garden when the flowers are dead." – Oscar Wilde

The following is the speech Jack prepared for sentencing. My understanding is all reference he makes to 1957 and 1958 are based on the FBI files he read over the course of a year, and not on memory. He did add more while speaking, but these were his prepared remarks:

*Jack McCullough reads his statement
to the Court before sentencing*

"Before I begin, I would like to thank my attorneys from the Public Defender's Office, Tom McCulloch and Robert Carlson, who have believed in me.

"Special thanks to investigator Crystal Harrolle, who went through all 4,000 pages of FBI documents to find the 15 pages of reports that proved my innocence in the Ridulph case. Yes, proved beyond a doubt that in 1957, I could not have been involved in the kidnap of Maria Ridulph. These reports were not even allowed to be referred to at trial.

"I would like to thank Janey O'Connor (my stepdaughter), who was here from Seattle to offer her support. She is my champion on the internet, in the media, and in my heart.

"I am deeply indebted to my wife and best friend, Sue, who has kept us from poverty and been my emotional anchor for the past 14 months of confinement.

"Your Honor and people of DeKalb County: I am Jack Daniel McCullough. I served in the Air Force, I am a former Army captain, police officer, and corporate vice president.

"Since my arrest in June 2011, I have been tried and declared guilty of the crime of kidnap and murder of Maria Ridulph. A crime I did not, would not, and could not have done.

"This is the oldest active cold case in American history. The kidnap occurred on December 3, 1957, about 7 p.m.

"The FBI interviewed approximately 1,800 suspects. Several suspects were of high interest, and one man was positively identified by the only eyewitness, Kathy Chapman. Thomas Rivard was identified on December 21, 1957, by Kathy Chapman in a lineup at a jail in Milwaukee, WI. The FBI filmed a movie of his appearance and then distributed the movie to area police departments and residents of Sycamore to view because he so strongly resembled the 'Johnny' of Kathy Chapman's 8-year-old memory. No one ever said it resembled me.

"I was well known in the town of Sycamore and in the local neighborhood. And, Kathy Chapman's father struck me with his car on April 1, 1947, as I was walking home from school to my residence on Center Cross Street.

"Because I was called 'Johnny' when I was young and because I lived a block and a half away from Maria Ridulph, I was interviewed, given a polygraph test, and thoroughly investigated and cleared by the FBI. The same FBI who later in my military career approved my Top Secret Crypto clearance for my position as an Army Intelligence Analyst.

"Now, 55 years later, by hearsay alone, I stand convicted of kidnap and murder.

"I didn't know just how good the FBI agents were until I read some of the 4,000 pages of discovery that were presented to my attorneys and investigator. However, one of my disappointments was to find out that the people who lived in my memory and in the FBI reports are now dead or senile. Only one of the witnesses that were important to my alibi is still alive. Colonel Theodore Liberwitz, who is 90 years old, lives in a nursing home and is a recent stroke victim. He is unable to recall my conversation with him that occurred on December 3, 1957, in the evening hours between 7:15 p.m. and 7:30 p.m. The second Air Force officer that I spoke with that evening, Technical Sergeant John Froom, is deceased.

"Everything I told the FBI and everyone I encountered on the evening of December 3, 1957, were interviewed and/ or investigated. The reports that were most important to me still exist and they verify that I placed a collect phone call from Rockford, IL at 6:57 p.m. to my dad, who answered the call at our residence in Sycamore, IL. The phone call lasted until 6:59 p.m., and it was verified by the collect call operator that my dad did, in fact, answer the call at our residence in Sycamore, IL. Dan Schaffer, the general manager for the Sycamore-Ogle Telephone Company, confirmed this call on December 9, 1957, when the FBI interviewed him.

"Colonel Liberwitz, Sgt. Froom, and the general manager of the telephone company confirm that I was in Rockford, IL on December 3, 1957, during the time that Maria Ridulph was kidnapped. Based on the FBI reports that were written at the time, Maria Ridulph was kidnapped at 7 p.m.

"Also included in the 4,000 pages of FBI reports are exact details of the descriptions that 8-year-old Kathy Chapman gave at the time of the kidnapping, the time of the kidnapping, and how the community responded.

"The FBI establishes that 'Johnny' contacted the two girls prior to 6:40 p.m., because according to Mrs. Ridulph's FBI statement, Maria retrieved her doll at 6:40 p.m. The FBI reports further establish that Maria Ridulph was last seen at 7 p.m., because Kathy Chapman asked 'Johnny' what time it was before she left to get her mittens and 'Johnny' replied 7 p.m. The police and neighbors were all in the streets by 8 p.m.

"These FBI reports were authored at the time of the disappearance; within them are the accurate details of the time, statements, and descriptions—unfortunately, the same does not hold true for Kathy Chapman and the other witnesses' memories.

"Your Honor, you partly based your guilty verdict on the testimony of two murderers and an undocumented

Mexican rapist. Their story was that I told them that I strangled Maria Ridulph. In the first place, why would I tell them anything when I have FBI documents that exonerate me? And secondly, none of the witnesses supported their claims. Not even the forensic expert who testified.

"Your Honor, you said that they knew things that only I could have told them and therefore, they were telling the truth. But there was a way for them to have inside information. John Doe and Chris Diaz's bunks were three feet from the telephone where I made calls every other day to my wife.

"Your Honor, I waived extradition to come to Illinois to clear my name. I gave a DNA sample voluntarily because I knew there could not have been a match. I knew that the FBI reports would prove again that I could not possibly have committed this crime. The prosecution has not proven anything beyond a reasonable doubt.

"Your Honor, many here are waiting for you to sentence me to life in prison. My question to you is, since when is life in prison the appropriate sentence for an innocent man? What purpose is served if you put an innocent man in prison? To sentence me, in the name of fairness and justice, you must look in the box!

"The FBI reports that you would not allow into trial show that I could not have been in both Sycamore and Rockford at the same time, and that time is 7 p.m., when it is documented that Maria Ridulph was kidnapped. Just because the witnesses who support my defense are all dead or senile doesn't mean that changes the facts! The state in this case has most definitely benefited from the passage of time! You ruled to keep the FBI reports out because of hearsay, but you failed to recognize that those reports should have been allowed in because they are both reliable and necessary.

"I have shown you the error of your judgment when it comes to the criminals' stories and alluded to multiple differences in 8-year-old Kathy Chapman's and the other witnesses' 1957 memories compared to their 2012 memories of the crime. You denied me the right to present the FBI reports that included all the facts and statements that exonerated me in 1957 and still should have exonerated me now in 2012."

- - -

After reading the sentencing and the above statements, you might ask yourself what exactly is in this FBI report that was not allowed to be used by the court? As well, why would the court not admit all the hard legwork and time investigating the crime, that it wouldn't be valuable in finding the truth to the missing and murdered girl, Maria Ridulph? If the FBI files equal the truth, then as a prosecutor, isn't that what you want, to find the truth and serve justice as it's meant to be? I have included the timeline put together by the FBI about the crime below for you to read and use your own judgment as to whether this would have helped and perhaps changed the outcome of the trial.

Let's compare the two stories that were reported on: first the FBI timeline and then the story that the court and media heard.

CHAPTER 4 — RETURN TO INNOCENCE

"Well, I was born in a small town, and I can breathe in a small town, gonna die in a small town, and that's probably where they'll bury me." John Mellencamp

I have included the FBI file timeline at the end of this book so that you will see what was known by the judge, prosecutor and even the defense, but it was not allowed in the trial as the judge considered the files hearsay. So, let's give you the story that was told to the court by witnesses, neighbors, and all people involved by the prosecution.

It was a typical winter day for December, when it was dusk by 4 p.m. and dark by 6 p.m. All the leaves had completely emptied from the trees and fallen onto the streets and sidewalks to the point that you could hardly see the pavement. It was December 3, 1957, and the forecast was for snow. This was to be winter's first strike of the year, and not the only first that night for the town of Sycamore.

Sycamore is a small rural community about 70 miles west of Chicago, Illinois, with a population of about 7,000 people. It really wasn't different from any other small town in the country, a place that people had moved to find the peace and relaxed setting that was without the rush and stress of the big city, and you knew who all your neighbors were. The city's main industry was marsh harvesting, which was part of its history dating back to 1859. This was a homey community that had farmers markets and pumpkin festivals, and people left their doors unlocked.

This was long before photos of missing children were put on milk cartons or the need to have an Amber Alert or Code Adam called over the PA system in a department store. These were the times that children walked to and from school every day and even talk to strangers on the street, as we were all told to respect our elders.

It was sometime in the 1940s that Michael and Frances Ridulph decided to move to Sycamore. They found the perfect house located at 616 Archie Street. It was a small rancher that was just a few blocks from West Elementary School. Michael worked at a wire and cable factory, one of the few factories in town, for $80 per week, while Frances was a homemaker. They attended the Evangelical Lutheran Church of St. John and had four children: the oldest was Charles, who was born in 1946; followed by three girls, Patricia, Kay, and the youngest, Maria.

Maria Ridulph at her 5th Birthday party

Maria was quite pretty, 3 feet 8 inches tall with big brown eyes and shoulder length curly hair and weighing about 53 pounds. In September of 1957, she started the second grade in school and was very intelligent. In fact, her best friend, Kathy Sigman, was starting grade three that year. Maria found the older kids much more interesting to talk with than the other girls that were her own age; to Maria, they just seemed too childish.

The first Tuesday in December that year started out like any other day. Maria and Kathy walked the short way to school that morning filled with the excitement of snow. So excited they were that they cut out paper snowflakes. On their way home from school around 4 p.m. that day, a strange man had approached them and started to ask them questions. Not being interested in what the man was saying to them, they laughed at him and went into a restaurant to have soda. When they left, the man had moved on, but scattered on the sidewalk outside of the restaurant were nude photos of women.

The girls always stopped at their favorite play spot on the corner of Archie Street and Center Cross Street. This was a regular stop for them throughout the summer. This time, it was going to be different. This time, there had been chalk-scrawled obscenities across the Elm tree. This shocked the girls, as it was not something that you would ever see in a small town like Sycamore anywhere, never mind on the trees where they liked to play.

After seeing the pictures drawn on the trees, they quickly started to run home, and while they were running, they quickly made plans to meet after dinner. They were so focused on the chance of snow and being able to play out in it for the first time this year, they soon forgot about what they had seen.

It was 5 p.m. sharp when the girls got back to their homes. Maria's family always gathered around the table for dinner. It was a time when the American family lived with more structure. The father went to work every day, as one person in the family could make enough to support a home. Mother would be a full-time homemaker, taking care of the kids, laundry, and cooking. Tonight, they would have another great meal for dinner. Roasted rabbit, carrots, potatoes, and milk.

Maria wolfed down two rabbit legs and got up from the table all excited, as she could see that it was beginning to snow outside. "Can I be excused?" Everybody at the table stopped what they were doing. "It's snowing out, can I go outside and play?" Her mother rolled her eyes and told Maria that it was okay, but to wash her hands first, and make sure that she was dressed warmly.

Maria's mother had never let her go out to play after dinner in winter; after all, it was dark and cold outside. This time, it seemed different to her. Almost like Maria had a purpose for going out and appeared much more eager than usual. Maria did not play outside much in winter, as she was not an outdoorsy type of girl. In the summer, Maria played outside with the other children, but it was also still very light after dinner.

Maria ran to the phone that was in a hallway near the kitchen. In 1957, most homes only had one dial phone and it was usually a party line where several families in a block would share the line. So, when you picked up the phone to talk, there could be another party in your block making a call at the same time. There was nobody on the line, so she dialed Kathy's house. "I can go outside tonight, can you?" It wouldn't be too long before they would meet at the same place on the corner of Center Cross Street and Archie Place, where the obscenities had been carved on the trees.

Maria then asked her mother if she would have to wear her shabby-looking tan overcoat, which a hand-me-down from her older brother, Chuck. Maria was embarrassed by the old jacket, as her friend Kathy always had nice, new clothes to wear that were bought for Kathy directly, not handed down to her like Maria's were. Maria's mother told her that if she were going to go out, she would wear her old jacket; she was not to wear her new jacket. So, Maria dressed in her used clothes and headed to the corner where she was to meet Kathy.

Kathy Sigman was 8 years old and lived down the block in a white house with a long driveway. Her family was also the very first in the area to own an electric clothes dryer. Every time that Kathy would go out to play, she was in freshly washed and dried clothes. They were still warm to the touch. She quickly got dressed and headed out to meet Maria.

The girls liked to play a game that they called "duck the cars," where they would run back and forth between the trees and street poles and onto the road just long enough for the driver of the car to see the color of their jackets in their headlights, while trying to avoid the oncoming cars. After greeting each other and talking about the freshly covered with snow road, they saw the first car coming down the road and started to take turns running out onto the street and quickly back to the sidewalk, laughing and screaming with joy. It was an oil truck, which parked on the corner of Center Cross Street and Archie Place, right at the neighbors', the Cliffes, house. A man got out of the truck and approached the house. He must be there to deliver oil to the house.

Within a few minutes, another car's headlights, but this time it was coming from Archie Place, where Maria lived. So, they started to run back onto the road to continue to play their game. The car that slowed to pass them both carefully was Maria's mother, who was taking her older sister, Kay, to her music lessons. As her mother glared at her through the passenger side of the car, both girls got real quiet and started to walk slowly on the sidewalk toward the corner, knowing that they were not supposed to behave that way and especially in the dark. As soon as Maria's mother drove out of sight, they ran back onto the road and started to giggle.

By about 6:15 p.m., Maria's mother was driving back home from dropping off Kay to her music lesson and saw the girls still playing on the corner of the road. She slowed the car down again as she drove by them and both girls waved and called out to her. Frances arrived back home and finished cleaning up the kitchen after dinner. She then went to her first-floor bedroom and started to read the newspaper.

By about 6:40 p.m., Maria had come into the bedroom and told her mother that she wanted her doll. Frances wanted to know what she was going to do with the doll and which doll she wanted. Maria mentioned her brand-new doll that she had just gotten in September when she was about to start second grade at school. Again, Frances told Maria not to take the new doll and told her that she should take one of her older dolls. Maria then left her bedroom and went into the living room where the dolls were all kept in a large wooden box. She started to rummage through the box and grabbed a doll. Her father was in the living room watching a western program on the television and didn't pay much attention to her. Her other sister, Patricia, was sitting at the dining room table doing her homework. She stopped and looked up at Maria to see what she was doing, but said nothing. Maria then took her doll and left the house without saying a word to anybody else.

It was only about five minutes later that Maria's friend, Kathy, came to the side door and knocked. Maria's brother, Chuck, who was playing records with the neighbor, Randy Strombom, answered the door. "I can't find Maria!" Kathy exclaimed. Chuck told Kathy that Maria was not in the house, so Kathy left.

It was only about another five minutes when Kathy came back to the door. Again, Chuck answered, and she told him that Maria was lost. Chuck went and told his mother, who in turn went into the living room and told Mr. Ridulph.

A few minutes later that Mr. Ridulph went out onto their front porch and called out Maria's name. Shortly after that, Mrs. Ridulph put on her heavy coat and joined him. They both walked to the sidewalk calling her name, slowly walking to the corner of Center Cross Street and Archie Place, where the girls were last seen playing, while continuing to call out Maria's name with no answer. At the corner, they ran into Kathy, who now had her 11-year-old brother, Edward, with her. They all continued to call out Maria's name, but got no answer. Shortly after this, Kathy and her brother headed back to their own home.

The Ridulphs walked back to their house. While Mr. Ridulph searched through their backyard, Mrs. Ridulph went inside and phoned Kathy Sigman's mother to inquire if Maria had been there. Mrs. Sigman told her that she was not, but that her own children had come back home. Frances now had a strange sense of fear run through her body and a strong ache come over her stomach, as she stared out their living room window. She telephoned Kathy Sigman's mother again and it was then that Mrs. Sigman told Frances about the man named "Johnny" who had been playing with Maria and Kathy earlier that evening, but knew nothing else.

CHAPTER 5 —
DON'T GIVE UP

"Sometimes, only one person is missing, and the whole world seems depopulated." – Alphonse de Lamartine

It was then that Maria's brother, Chuck, and his friend, Randy, who had been listening to records with him earlier that evening, took flashlights and headed out to search the streets for Maria. While Mr. Ridulph was still searching outside, Mrs. Ridulph headed across the street to their neighbor, William Lindstrom, to see if he knew or heard anything. While she was heading back to their house, Frances had a flash of how Maria had often played with a boy named John who lived on Roosevelt Court, a dead-end street parallel to Archie Place. She quickly got into her car, backed it out of the driveway, and stopped to pick up her husband, who was still out on the road searching. He got in and she quickly explained where she was headed.

After they arrived at their destination, Mr. Ridulph got out of his car with a whistle and started whistling for Maria. He could see into the front window of Maria's friend John's house, and only saw two ladies watching television, so he didn't disturb them. He jumped into the car and they took off to DeKalb Avenue, where they soon saw Patricia, their daughter, and Chuck with Randy, who had run into each other while searching for Maria. Mr. Ridulph opened his car window and asked them if they found out anything. Their response was no, so he told them to get into the car.

They quickly all got back into the car circled the block and drove down Fair Street, where the school grounds were located. They circled the block twice, but there was no sign of Maria, so they drove back home.

By the time that they arrived home, their other daughter, Kay, was there, as she just got back from her music lessons from earlier that night. She was not aware of Maria's disappearance. By this time, some of the other neighbors who were aware of Maria's disappearance were out searching also. Mrs. Ridulph walked into the house and the first thing she did was pick up the phone to call Kathy's mother again. This time, she wanted to find out from Kathy what Maria had taken outside with her, which was just her doll. It was now that Mrs. Sigman mentioned to her about the man that was giving the girls piggyback rides. Again, Mrs. Ridulph just dismissed it and decided to finally report the disappearance to the police.

It was about 7:50 p.m. when Mrs. Ridulph drove to the police station, taking her daughter Patricia with her. But on the way to the police station, they decided to drive past a creek on Mill Street on the chance that Maria might have gone there to play. They drove to the lumberyard on Grant Street as well, to see if by chance Maria was playing on the woodpiles. After finding no trace of Maria, they made it to the police station and reported Maria's disappearance.

The police dispatched police cars to the Ridulphs' home as well as drove around their neighborhood. While talking to the police, Mrs. Ridulph said that she had not reported Maria's disappearance earlier as her husband talked her out of it. You see, Maria had wandered off before about a year earlier and caused a great deal of commotion. It was embarrassing, as Maria came home a few hours later. She had been out playing and lost track of time. Mrs. Ridulph then grabbed Patricia and left the police station, remembering that in the previous year, Maria had gone to the Elmwood

Cemetery and was gone long enough that the same thing happened with all the neighbors and police were out looking for her. Maria finally returned later that night. So, off to the Elmwood Cemetery they went, again with no luck.

When Mrs. Ridulph arrived back home, the police were there and wanted to ask her a few questions about Kathy and Kathy's parents, the Sigmans. Mrs. Ridulph said that the two girls had been friends for a few years and have had no real problems. She knew the Sigmans, but only because the two daughters were close; they were not social with them at all. Most of the time, the girls played at the Ridulphs' house; the Sigmans didn't allow the girls to play inside their house, as the girls would just get the place dirty.

December 1957
Maria Ridulph goes missing.
The search continues for months.

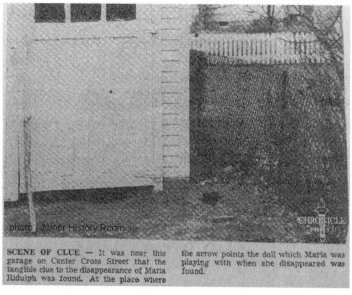

SCENE OF CLUE — It was near this garage on Center Cross Street that the tangible clue to the disappearance of Maria Ridulph was found. At the place where the arrow points the doll which Maria was playing with when she disappeared was found.

*December 1957 Newspaper brief about
the search for Maria Ridulph*

Frances also remembered that when she was taking her daughter Kay to her music lessons earlier that evening, she had to drive around an oil delivery truck that was parked on the corner of Center Cross Street and Archie Place in front of the Cliffe home. When she returned after dropping her daughter off, the truck had gone already.

Following that information, the police found out that Mr. Tom Braddy was the Standard Oil bulk dealer in Sycamore and sent an officer by his house to interview him on what, if anything, he saw while doing the oil delivery to the Cliffe house that evening.

When officers D. Fraher and R. Bales arrived to Braddys' house, they commented in their report that Braddy appeared reliable and sincere. He stated that he was most anxious to see the case come to a successful end. He stated further that he was delivering oil to the Cliffe home earlier that evening at the corner of Center Cross Street and Archie Place, was finished and gone by 6:15 p.m., passed a service station clock by 6:20 p.m. on his way back to the bulk station where he left his tank truck, and headed for home in his pickup truck to have dinner.

It was there at about 7:10 p.m. that he received a phone call from Mrs. Cliffe, who asked him if he had seen any stranger with the Ridulph girl while he was making the oil delivery. He replied to her that he had only seen the girls and no stranger. He then offered to come out and help in the search. He and his son, Dale, headed to the corner of Center Cross Street and Archie Place, where he had last seen the girls, which was only about two and a half blocks from his home.

They had run into Bud Sigman, Kathy's father, and the three of them walked south on Center Cross Street until they came to the Johnson house. It was there that they noticed two sets of footprints: one belonging to an adult, and the other belonging to a child. Dale compared his own shoe to the adult footprint, which to him appeared to be a size 9. The prints led up to the Johnson garage, where the last adult print appeared to show a sharp movement to the right, such as an adult picking up a child or perhaps throwing something like a doll. The three of them had attached so much importance to these prints that Braddy sent Bud Sigman and Dale to surround the garage quickly, thinking that they might find him, but there was nobody there. They continued their search and at the edge of the street, noticed fresh tire tracks in the snow, indicating that someone had pulled in and out sharply, going north toward Route 64.

CHAPTER 6 — SEEING IS BELIEVING

"My dear friend, clear your mind of can't." – Samuel Johnson

Maria Ridulph with her best friend Kathy Sigmund

It wasn't until the next day that the police sat down with Kathy Sigman to try to detail the events of the evening before. She remembered how excited that the two girls were as it was the first snowfall of the year. Kathy's parents were a little better off financially than the Ridulphs were. Her mother would never allow them to play in the Sigman house, as she was worried that the girls would just get the house dirty. So, they had to play outside or in their unheated garage. It was now winter and not very fun to be stuck in the garage with Dad's car, and they didn't like to play outside in the dark unless there was snow. So, they would usually end up at Maria's house. The snow was like magic, transforming the outside yards and roads into a fantastic journey. They could imagine all sorts of things happening when the outside glowed from the snow-covered ground.

They met that night at the corner of Center Cross Street and Archie Place, where they had seen the dirty drawings carved onto the trees earlier that day. When they arrived, they were both so excited it was snowing and giggling as they tried to catch snowflakes with their tongues. It was then that they saw the oil truck delivery man drive up to the corner to make his oil delivery to the Cliffe house. As soon as they saw the truck lights heading toward them, they both started to play their favorite game, "duck the cars." Running in and out of the road between the poles and trees, they couldn't stop laughing. Soon the oil truck passed them and stopped at the Cliffe house, and the driver got out of the truck and started to make his delivery.

The girls quickly ran back to the intersection of the two roads jumping and skipping through the snow-covered sidewalks.

Again, there was another set of car lights heading toward them, so quickly, they got back into position to start playing their game again. Only then, Maria noticed that it was her own mother's car, so quickly she screamed at Kathy and they both ran back to the sidewalk. As the car drove by them, it slowed to a crawl. Looking through the passenger window was her mother, shaking her hand at the girls as if to tell them to stop playing on the road. Then she continued to drive back at regular speed, as she was taking her daughter, Kay, to her music lessons.

As Frances Ridulph's car got out of sight of the two girls, Kathy remembers a good-looking young man approach them. He had blonde hair that was swept back into a ducktail, a gap in his teeth, and was wearing a colorful sweater. Kathy also remembered his big teeth and high, thin voice. She had never seen him before. "Hello, little girls," he said. "Are you having fun?"

He told them his name was Johnny and asked whether they wanted piggyback rides. He then told them that he was 24 and not married. This seems to be a strange thing for someone to mention on the street like that. He then asked the girls if they liked dollies. Both girls nodded yes.

The stranger named Johnny picked up Maria on his back and ran up Center Cross Street about 20 feet, then back again. Maria giggled with glee while on his shoulders; Johnny had won her over.

When it was over, Maria ran to her house at 616 Archie Place to get her doll for the next piggyback ride. Kathy waited on the sidewalk with Johnny, and it was then that he asked her if she wanted to take a walk around the block or go for a trip in a truck, car, or bus. No, she told him. He told her that she was pretty, but Kathy sensed that Johnny like Maria better than her.

Soon, Maria came back with a rubber doll and joined them on the sidewalk. It was now Kathy's turn to run home, to get her mittens. She asked Maria to come along with her, but she didn't want to go. Kathy then ran to her home for her mittens. When she returned a few minutes later, both Johnny and Maria were gone.

Kathy started by calling out Maria's name. There was just silence. All she could hear was the snow lightly falling all around her. Kathy then started running up and down the street, at first lightly calling out Maria's name, but her voice started to get louder and louder as the panic set in. At first, her fear was that Maria was having fun with Johnny without her, but slowly, that jealous nature turned into real fear for Maria.

Kathy then rushed up to the side door at the Ridulphs' house and knocked. Maria's big brother, Chuck, answered. "I can't find Maria," she told him. Chuck and his friend, Randy, were playing records on their hi-fi, and he was a little bothered by the intrusion. He responded, "She's not here." Kathy then put her head down and returned to the road to continue her search, only to return to the Ridulph house again.

"She's lost. I can't find Maria," Kathy blurted out.

"Hold on," Chuck replied. He walked back into the house to the first-floor bedroom where his mother was reading the newspaper and told her what was happening. She put her paper down with no care for keeping her page, went into the living room and told Mr. Ridulph. He got up out of his chair and walked toward the side door, when he ran into Chuck and asked him to go out and look for his sister.

Chuck and Randy put on jackets and shoes and each grabbed a flashlight and headed outside to find Maria.

The boys started down Archie Place calling out Maria's name, heading toward Center Cross Street, then to the elementary school. When they reached the elementary school, the two boys saw a police car go by, but realized too late that they should have stopped it. They then headed back home.

By then, Kathy had gone home and told her mother of the events that had happened earlier in the evening. Kathy then returned to help search for Maria, and this time, she had her brother with her. They walked up and down the streets calling out her name. It seemed like they had been walking forever, and finally had to give up as it was so cold now and getting late, so they headed back home.

The police continued canvassing the neighbors for any information they could find. The first bit of information they received was from neighbors Kenneth Davy and Mr. and Mrs. Roy Peifer, who had seen Maria and Kathy playing on the corner of Center Cross Street and Archie Place at approximately 6:30 p.m.

The next report they received was from Mrs. Stanley Wells, another neighbor, who recalled looking out her window between 6:30 p.m. and 7 p.m. and seeing two children playing with an adult. She couldn't tell if the adult was male or female. Then, at about 7 p.m., she heard a shriek and looked out her window again, but could not see anyone.

Another neighbor, Elmer Westburn, also heard a scream at about 7 p.m. and looked out his window, but could not see anyone, either. Another concern was brought to the attention of the investigators when Mrs. Meredith Strombom found Maria's doll about two feet from the Johnsons' garage between 8 p.m. and 9 p.m., which was after the searchers who had been through earlier, finding the footprints on the driveway of the same house, had searched. There was no doll then.

After a two-week police investigation, canvassing of neighbors, and several people of the town of Sycamore searching the area, a 20-square-mile search was conducted using helicopters and planes on December 19, which also produced nothing. Interviews were then conducted on anybody who had received parking tickets or who was observed in the area, which turned up nothing as well.

The detectives then brought Kathy into the police station to show her photographs of various former inmates of many mental and penal institutions. She could not identify any of them as Johnny.

There were no extortion calls, letters, or demands received.

CHAPTER 7 — JUST BELIEVE IN DESTINY

"Life is 10% what happens to you and 90% how you react to it." – Charles R. Swindoll

On the evening of December 3, 1957, men pounded on the door of 227 Center Cross Street, the home of Ralph and Eileen Tessier. Ralph ran the hardware store in Sycamore. The men wanted him to open, even though it was after hours of regular business, as they needed to gather up flashlights and lanterns to use in the search for Maria.

The Tessiers were a large family who had lived in a small house only two blocks from the Ridulphs. Eileen was Ralph's Irish-born war bride who had sailed to the U.S. on the Queen Mary with her son, John, from a previous marriage. Together, the couple would have six of their own children: Katherine, Jeanne, Mary Pat, Bob, Janet, and Nancy.

The five sisters resented their brother John. He seemed to get away with anything that he felt like doing. He was 18, and considered himself artistic, but they just thought that he was lazy. He would get into problems at school all the time. If he even showed up for class, it wouldn't be on time, and he certainly didn't give his teachers any respect. In fact, he was even expelled once for pushing his teacher and calling her a bitch. But their mother would always praise John no matter what trouble he got into.

As soon as Ralph Tessier heard of the missing Maria, he joined the search for her. Eileen headed for the armory, where a command center for the search had been set up. It was there that she got all the women organized, making sandwiches and coffee for the searchers. The Tessiers left their children at home and had even locked their front door, which they had never done before; in fact, none of them could even find the key for the front door as nobody could remember when they last had locked the door. At that time, nobody knew where John was.

In the next couple of days while the police were canvassing the neighborhood, they came to the Tessiers' residence again. This time, they questioned Eileen about the events of December 3. The older girls just sat and listened, saying nothing. One thing that they heard that made them all look at each other was when their mother told the detective that their brother John had been home all night on the 3. The girls all knew that it wasn't true. None of them had seen him for a few days.

It was only a matter of two days before the FBI decided to get involved in the case, as they thought that perhaps Maria was abducted and taken across state lines. The FBI interviewed many witnesses who had seen the two girls playing without any other person present between 6 p.m. and 6:30 p.m. and spoke to family members who had seen or spoken to Maria and Kathy during Maria getting her doll and Kathy getting her mittens. Based on these interviews, "Johnny" was thought to have approached the girls after 6:30 p.m., and the FBI concluded that Maria was abducted between 6:45 p.m. and 7 p.m.

Kathy Sigman was the only witness who had seen "Johnny" and was placed in protective custody, as the police and FBI feared that the kidnapper would return to harm her. John Tessier was on the original list of suspects based on a tip, but the police failed to have Kathy identify him after he provided an alibi for the night of the crime.

In late December of 1957, Kathy was then taken to the Dane County Sheriff's Office in Madison, Wisconsin, to see a lineup of possible suspects. She positively identified Thomas Joseph Rivard, who was described in the FBI documents as a 35-year-old man approximately 5 feet, 4 inches tall and weighing 156 pounds, with dark blond wavy, bushy hair. However, it was discovered afterward that he had a solid alibi, as he was in jail at the time of the kidnapping. The FBI had suspected somebody else that was in the same line up as Rivard, and he was just there to fill out the lineup. It should also be said that Rivard did not physically resemble John Tessier, who was six inches taller and 17 years younger than Rivard. Also, when asked several years after the lineup, Kathy said that she didn't remember picking Rivard out of a lineup.

Maria's disappearance had received national news coverage by now, and both President Dwight D. Eisenhower and FBI Director J. Edgar Hoover took an interest in the case. Maria's parents even appeared on television and in other media pleading for their daughter's safe return and the public's help in finding her.

CHAPTER 8 — EXTRA! EXTRA! READ ALL ABOUT IT

"Boldly going where hundreds have gone before does not make headlines." – Neil deGrasse Tyson

Headlines of the kidnapping of Maria Ridulph

The headline on the front page of Sycamore's afternoon paper screamed the bad news that everybody in town already suspected: "Missing Girl, 7, Feared Kidnapped." Foul play was suspected, but there were no real clues. When Maria went missing, she was wearing a brown three-quarter length coat, black corduroy slacks, brown socks, and freshly polished saddle shoes. She weighed about 55 pounds, was 44 inches tall and wore her hair in a wavy brown bob style with bangs.

The man who called himself Johnny, police reported, wore a striped sweater of blue, yellow, and green. He had long blond hair that curled in the front and flopped onto his forehead.

But there were conflicting reports about the exact time of Maria's disappearance. Was she snatched closer to 6 p.m. or did it happen later, at about 7 p.m.? Police and FBI reports as well as newscasts from the time contained details that supported both scenarios.

Sycamore's police chief, William Hindenburg, told FBI agents that Kathy and Maria went out to play at 6:02 p.m., but the DeKalb County sheriff said that Maria didn't call Kathy to ask her to come out and play until 6:30 p.m. Maria's mother later altered her original estimate, saying the girls could have been outside as early as 10 minutes to 6. The time differences would become a very important matter when the case was reopened 50 years later.

After a week had passed, Maria's mother decided to go to the media and make a plea for her daughter. "God forgives mistakes. We would, too," Frances Ridulph said to the local newspaper reporter. "Maria was a nervous girl, a nail biter who could quickly become hysterical if things didn't go her way." She continued, "Maria would make a noise if something seemed wrong, and no kidnapper would put up with that for long." She exclaimed, "Whoever took her away hit her weak spot. He played with her." The frantic mother finished.

Frances then went to the local TV station to deliver a message to Maria. "Don't cry, Maria. Above all, don't cry. Don't make a fuss. We'll be with you soon."

While Frances was using the media to help try to find Maria, Maria's father, Michael, scolded the reporters who were camped out at the police station. "For God's sake, quit saying she is dead. I know she is still alive. Nobody would have any reason to kill her." He then pulled one reporter out from the crowd and explained, "I want fathers to help look for my little girl."

Chuck Ridulph went along with his father to the fire station on the morning of December 4 and was assigned to a search team. There were hundreds of people who fanned out over the fields surrounding Sycamore. Others would go around opening car doors and checking people's cellar doors. "People were even carrying guns," Chuck said. In a neighborhood called Johnson's Greenhouse, where new streets had been going in, Chuck was asked to climb down a manhole because he was the only one in the search party small enough to fit. He found a sack full of abandoned kittens, which unnerved Chuck. Other searchers found a torn, bloody petticoat in a farm field, but it was not Maria's.

Meanwhile, back at the Ridulph home, two FBI agents took up residence in the living room. This is where they would organize more search groups. The Illinois State Police set up a half a dozen roadblocks and searched all motel rooms, railroad cars, and the bus station.

Maria's doll that was discovered near the Johnson home was shipped to an FBI lab near Washington for analysis. So were her schoolbooks, hairbrush, a toy oven, tin saxophone, and her records of songs including "The Farmer in the Dell."

Kathy Sigman was now under the 24-hour protection of a police guard, while the family doctor checked her over for signs of any sexual molestation. Kathy's mother then bent down and placed her hands on Kathy's shoulders, looked directly in her eyes, and said, "You have to remember his face because you're the only one who can catch him. You are the only one who knows what he looks like."

They found exactly nothing! There was no ransom note, no phone calls from the kidnapper.

Authorities now believed that Maria's abductor had a twisted motive. He was a sexual predator. The police chief was certain nobody from Sycamore would do such a thing. It had to be the work of a trucker or someone else passing through. The FBI wasn't so sure, as its investigation revealed that there was no shortage of potential suspects in town. Hindenburg, the police chief, told reporters that he had rounded up and questioned all known sexual deviants, local peeping toms, and followed tips about two men called "Commando" and "Mr. X." After weeks of searching without finding anything, police alerted residents to look out for scavengers, as it was possible that Maria's body was dumped in a nearby field or on a farm, to be alert to large gatherings of buzzards and crows, and if a body was located, to make sure nothing was touched.

The FBI was running out of funds to cover the investigation. Its temporary office in Sycamore had been functioning for two weeks with a cost of $3,600 per diem for 29 agents. The supervisor had written a report on December 15, 1957, to Hoover, explaining that they had tracked down 250 leads and processed 200 suspects, all with negative results. Agents still had about 125 leads to go. The Chicago G-men all found it most peculiar that such a rigorous investigation had turned up nothing. The locals had passed on tips about all their homosexuals, queers, and fairies when the FBI was looking for sex deviants of a different kind. Agents were hampered by the sheer volume of leads, leading to this observation: "I have never seen a city as small as Sycamore with such a large volume of these unusual individuals."

Hoover responded, urging them to keep going, saying, "This case must receive continuous, aggressive, imaginative, investigative attention."

The best evidence they had was from Kathy Sigman. Some of her details varied, such as whether Johnny had a missing tooth in the front or if it was just a gap, but she never wavered from the core facts. The agent who questioned her had described her as completely mature and seemingly fearless during questioning and police lineups; she always stayed steadfast.

Christmas was a very somber holiday for Sycamore. The local papers even ran a large photo of Maria's family sitting by their Christmas tree. Her mother had bought Maria a typewriter and even wrapped her other gifts and put them under the tree. Shortly before Christmas, the agents had all packed up and gone home for the holidays with no new developments. Soon, the story dropped from the headlines, but the town people remained on edge. It was no longer the small, quaint town where you would help an older lady across the street, or a stranger who was a man could walk down an alley without the police being called.

The city then decided to cut down the elm tree on the corner of Archie Place and Center Cross Street. People could disappear in a large city, but not in a small town like Sycamore.

It was April 26, 1958, near Woodbine, Illinois, about 100 miles from Sycamore, when two tourists searching for morel mushrooms in a wooded area along Route 20 discovered the skeletal remains of a small child, wearing only a shirt, undershirt, and socks, under a partially fallen tree. The farm that she was found on was owned by Roy Cahill. Birds and animals had fed on her corpse.

The decomposed condition of the body indicated it had been there for several months. The body was identified as Maria Ridulph based on dental records, a lock of hair, and the shirts and socks she had been wearing when she disappeared. The rest of Maria's clothing, including her coat, slacks, shoes, and an undergarment, was not found. No photographs were taken of the crime scene, although photos were taken of the general location without showing the body, because the coroner, James Furlong, did not want photos of the child's body leaked to newspapers. Because the crime had occurred within Illinois rather than crossing state lines, the FBI withdrew from the case, leaving local and state police to solve the case.

At the coroner's inquest, the tourist, Frank A. Sitar, a retired man from Minnesota, described the scene he encountered that spring afternoon. "I thought it was an old deer hide. I came up to it then and I could see some bones and I thought somebody had shot a dog. Then I looked closer, and it looked like human bones. I noticed the jacket, but I didn't pay any attention to it until I noticed the skull. Then I started to look further, and I noticed the hair. And I saw then that it was a little girl." He walked back to the car and told his wife. They then drove to the farmhouse and called the police.

The initial autopsy did not determine the cause of death due to the state of decomposition. During an autopsy done 50 years later, a forensic anthropologist determined Maria had likely been stabbed several times in the throat.

Maria was laid to rest in a small white casket on a warm spring day. An overflow crowd of at least 300 filled the Evangelical Lutheran Church of St. John in Sycamore. Kathy was at the funeral, still under police guard at that time.

"This little girl has entered into everlasting peace, probably on the night she was taken," said Rev. Louis L. Going. "Maria was taken out of life through unusual circumstances, but nothing could deprive her of her God-given salvation." The organist then played "Jesus Loves Me," which was Maria's favorite hymn.

WORDS FROM THE PAST

Maria Ridulph was the youngest of four children, with two older sisters and one older brother. One of her sisters, Kay, who recently passed away, had left her diary behind for her older brother, Chuck, to read. Chuck let the CBS news crew use the diary for a television special.

"December 3, 1957, Tuesday, when I came home at 7:30 I was informed that Maria was kidnapped. It didn't really hit me until we found her doll by the garage. The whole town formed a searching party, which continued throughout the whole night.

"All those FBI guys are so nice, just before supper I got fingerprinted by the FBI. I wished Maria could have been here to go through this, she would have enjoyed so many things, getting fingerprinted by the FBI and all."

"December 8, 1957, in church reverend sang a hymn for Maria, I couldn't take it, I started crying, you could hear sobs all over the church. Helicopters were flying around looking for Maria, I'm glad they didn't find anything."

"December 11, 1957, in tonight's paper it told everyone to look for a flock of crows or buzzards because they would be eating on the body, of all the nerve."

"Mother made a film for TV pleading with her kidnapper, just please bring her back! Please bring her back.

"December 25, 1957, Christmas Wednesday, at Grandpa's everyone said a prayer for Maria. Chuck is taking it like a good soldier, he doesn't say anything, just listens. He'll take it the hardest."

"April 26, 1958 Saturday, I went to my lessons at 6:45 then father Duvine came, he told us that a body was found, and it didn't hit me yet, and I started crying with the boys standing there.

"She was decomposed down to the skeleton, except for where she had her cloths on, the cause of death is not known yet, but its very evident our waiting is over."

Kay passed away on September 26, 2011.

CHAPTER 9 — BACK TO GOOD

"Some memories are unforgettable, remaining ever vivid and heartwarming." – Joseph B. Wirthlin

McCullough Family in 1944

John Tessier was born John Cherry on November 27, 1939, in Belfast, Northern Ireland, to British Sgt. Samuel Cherry and his wife, Eileen McCullough. Samuel Cherry was killed early in World War 2. During the war, Eileen Cherry served as one of the first female spotters with the UK's Royal Air

Force and met Ralph Tessier, who was serving with the U.S. 8th Army Air Force at RAF Bovingdon, England. She married Ralph Tessier in November 1944, and she and her son John, who was then aged 5 moved to Sycamore, Illinois, where Ralph and Eileen had six more children together over the years. After his mother's marriage to Ralph, John took the last name of Tessier, although he was sometimes still called John Cherry.

John Tessier told FBI investigators that on the night of December 3, 1957, he was in Rockford, Illinois, which is approximately 40 miles northwest of Sycamore, to enlist in the Air Force. Now, if you remember, this story differed from his mother's story, who had told the local police that John was home all night long.

John said that he had been in Chicago on December 2 and 3, undergoing physical examinations that were required for his enlistment. On the morning of December 3, he had visited the Chicago recruiting station, which was later corroborated by records. John then spent the rest of the day sightseeing in Chicago before returning to Rockford by train that evening, which arrived at 6:45 p.m.

Upon his arrival in Rockford, he called his parents to ask for a ride home to Sycamore. Telephone records were later found to show a collect call was placed from the Rockford post office to the Tessier home at 6:57 p.m. that evening by someone who called himself "John Tessier" as written down by the operator.

After making that call, Tessier then met with officers from the Rockford recruiting station to drop off the paperwork relating to his enlistment. The officers confirmed that they spoke with John at about 7:15 p.m. that evening, although one of the officers had expressed some concerns about John's credibility and conduct.

Tessier was brought to the police station to take a lie detector test, which he passed. In view of his alibi and the lie detector result, Tessier was taken off the suspect list and the FBI closed out his report on December 10, 1957, noting: "No further investigation is being conducted regarding the above suspect." This is perhaps why Kathy Sigman never saw a photo of Tessier or saw him in a lineup. Tessier left Sycamore the next day to report for basic training at Lackland Air Force Base.

Tessier served in the U.S. military for 13 years and rose to the rank of captain. After leaving the service he moved to Seattle, Washington, where he subsequently graduated from King County Law Enforcement Academy in June 1974 and became a police officer in the small town of Lacey, Washington, which is near Olympia.

He later joined the police department in Milton, Washington, where he clashed with the chief of police, who attempted to fire him and documented a long list of complaints about his work and conduct.

In 1982, Tessier let a 15-year-old runaway girl, Michelle Weinman, and her friend, who knew him as a Milton police officer, stay in his home.

Weinman would later testify that that shortly after moving in with Tessier, he would fondle her and perform oral sex on her. Tessier was then charged with statutory rape, a felony. After plea negotiations, he pleaded guilty to communication with a minor for immoral purposes, a misdemeanor. He was sentence to one-year formal probation and was terminated from the Milton police force.

On April 27, 1994, John Tessier legally changed his name to Jack Daniel McCullough, saying that he wanted to honor his late mother. By 2011, McCullough, now in his early 70s, was living at a retirement community in the Northwest part of Seattle, where he worked as a security guard.

CHAPTER 10 — TRUTH BE TOLD ...

"Truth is everybody is going to hurt you. You just gotta find the ones worth suffering for." – Bob Marley

It should be known that Jack does not only believe that he was just wrongly arrested, charged, and later convicted for the murder of Maria Ridulph. He also wants everyone to know that there was a lot of corruption involved.

Before Jack discusses the officers who knowingly had him convicted wrongfully, he thinks it's very important for the public to be very proud of their men in blue for the dangerous job they do. At the time of this writing, some of the people who helped get Jack incarcerated wrongly are not only still working, but have also received raises and bonuses in their careers.

It is Jack's opinion that the Illinois State Police are covering up the misdeeds of Detective Brion Hanley. Jack claims that not only did Officer Hanley hide evidence, he lied to the grand jury that indicted Jack.

The next person on Jack's hit list is the former state's attorney, Clay Campbell, who he figures masterminded the conspiracy with Hanley to lie to the Seattle police detectives. This particular case is now in front of the courts, so details are not available.

Remember that the critical piece of evidence that convicted Jack also set him free. The evidence in question was where the pay phone was that Jack used to call his mother the night of the murder, and the time the call was placed. Hanley discovered that Jack made the phone call from a pay phone located at the Rockford post office, which was located at 401 S. Main Street, at 6:57 p.m. Maria was kidnapped between 6:45 and 6:55 p.m. This would make it impossible for Jack to have been in two places at one time, and he could not have taken Maria that night.

State Attorney Clay Campbell

Whether you believe that Hanley and Campbell both pursued Jack just because they thought he was guilty and were just fudging the evidence to make it work or, as Jack and his family believe, actually intended to put Jack away for a murder he didn't commit because of their corrupt morals, I leave to you, the reader, to decide. It doesn't really matter what the motives for their actions were, in either case, it's wrong and not what we expect from our law enforcement.

A great example of what we want from our prosecution is honorable behavior, such as what DeKalb County state's attorney Richard Schmack displayed when he reviewed the evidence of the case and presented the correct times to the court, which eventually got Jack released from prison.

Below are two suspects for the murder of Maria Ridulph

JOHNNY HILBURN

It is now Jack's belief that Johnny Hilburn, a Quaker Oat employee from Rockford, Illinois, is Maria Ridulph's killer. It was in the FBI files that Johnny had admitted to talking to two little girls at 6:30 p.m. on the night that Maria went missing, on the street that the two girls were playing on. He stated in the report that he was asking the girls for directions, even though he knew the area quite well.

Maria's body was later found dumped in the woods on the side of Route 20, the road that Johnny would take going home from work.

Johnny Hilburn was later convicted and spent time in Stateville prison for molesting his own 5-year-old daughter. It is quite often a question of Jack's as to why the FBI never acted on such evidence.

WILLIAM HENRY REDMOND

In 1997, Sycamore police Lt. Patrick Solar closed the then 40-year-old Ridulph case, naming William Henry Redmond, a former truck driver and carnival worker from Nebraska who had died in 1992, as the man who likely abducted and killed Maria Ridulph. Redmond had been charged in 1988 with a 1951 murder of an 8-year-old Pennsylvania girl, although the case was dismissed when a police officer refused to reveal the name of a confidential informant. Redmond was also suspected in the 1951 disappearance of 10-year-old Beverly Potts in Ohio. According to Solar, Redmond told a fellow inmate that he committed a crime like the Ridulph abduction and murder. Solar also believed that Redmond's appearance and behavior matched that of "Johnny." Solar's report was criticized due to lack of supporting evidence and alleged political motives. Solar himself acknowledged that the evidence against Redmond was circumstantial and that if Redmond had lived, it would have been difficult to convict him in the Ridulph case unless he confessed. For that reason,

Solar called the Ridulph case closed, but not solved, leaving open the possibility that a better suspect might be found. When Jack McCullough was tried in the Ridulph case, the trial judge ruled out any testimony about Redmond because he was not a credible suspect.

CHAPTER 11 — OPENING A CAN OF WORMS

The case was reopened in 2008 based on new information from McCullough's half-sister, Janet Tessier. According to Janet, their mother, Eileen Tessier, on her deathbed in January 1994 had said, "Those two little girls, and the one that disappeared, John did it. John did it, and you have to tell someone." Janet took that statement as meaning that her half-brother, John Tessier, soon to rename himself Jack McCullough, had kidnapped and murdered Maria Ridulph. Janet also heard from her older sisters, Katherine Tessier Caulfield and Jeanne Tessier, that Eileen had lied to investigators when she told them John was at home on the night of the crime.

Another of Jack's half-sisters, Mary Pat Tessier Hunt, was also present when their mother spoke to Janet, but later testified that she had only heard her mother say, "He did it." Nevertheless, Mary Pat testified that she had the same understanding as Janet and that her older sisters had suspected John of the murders for years.

At the time of her death, Eileen, a cancer patient, was on morphine and, according to her doctor, disoriented. Jack, who allegedly had once threatened to kill Janet with a gun and sexually molested his half-sister Jeanne when she was a minor, was estranged from the Tessier family by the time of Eileen's death. He was told not to attend her funeral.

Janet Tessier said that she made several attempts over the next 14 years to get law enforcement, including the

Sycamore police and the FBI, to consider her mother's deathbed statement. Patrick Solar, who was the lieutenant of the Sycamore police department at the time and had identified William Henry Redmond as the most likely suspect, told CNN that Janet had never spoken to him, but that he would never have suspected John because he knew the Tessier family. Ralph Tessier, Jack's father, had even painted the police cars for Sycamore, and John Tessier had been cleared by the FBI in 1957.

Janet Tessier (Jack's Half-Sister) and Captain Tony Arpacz

In 2008, Janet sent an email to the Illinois State tip line, resulting in the state police cold case unit undertaking a lengthy investigation into McCullough's background and alibi for the night of the murder. Janet's sisters, Katherine and Jeanne, told the investigators of their suspicions, and Jeanne also told them that Jack had molested her as a child as well as other young girls. Another woman alleged that John Tessier had given her a piggyback ride as a child and refused to put her down until her father intervened. State police investigators reviewed evidence and developed a new timeline under which Tessier could have kidnapped Maria and driven to Rockford in time to make the phone call at 6:57 p.m. to his mother, and then meet with the recruiting officers at 7:15 p.m. Under the new timeline, they determined that Maria would have been kidnapped no later than 6:20 p.m. The police search was underway by 7 p.m., according to Katherine, who said that she came home from a party that night at 7 p.m. and the search was already in progress.

Hoping to have Kathy Sigman review a photographic lineup, police took five pictures from the 1957 Sycamore high school yearbook, but John Tessier's picture was not in the yearbook as he had been expelled for pushing his teacher. Police then obtained a contemporary photo of him from his former girlfriend, which differed from the photos in the yearbook in that Tessier was wearing an open collar rather than a suit and the background was dark rather than light. Sigman identified the picture of Tessier as Johnny.

Along with the picture, Tessier's former girlfriend also provided an unused military-issued train ticket from Rockford to Chicago dated December 1957. The investigators took this to suggest that contrary to Tessier's alibi, Tessier had not taken the train on his trip to Chicago and had instead driven his car there, meaning that he could have driven back to Sycamore after noon on December 3, kidnapped Maria, and driven to Rockford. The police located a high school friend of Tessier's who recalled seeing Tessier's distinctively painted car in Sycamore that afternoon and said that Tessier did not let anyone else drive his car.

In July of 2011, the Seattle Police Department, which had now joined the Illinois State Police in the investigation, brought McCullough in for questioning, using a professional interrogator due to his law enforcement experience.

At first, McCullough spoke calmly and cooperated, but when faced with questions about the murder of Maria Ridulph and his whereabouts on the night of the crime, he became evasive and aggressive. After McCullough refused to answer any more questions, he was arrested for the kidnapping and murder of Maria Ridulph and extradited to Illinois.

CHAPTER 12 —
INTERROGATION

On June 29, 2011, 72-year-old former policeman Jack McCullough was taken into the Seattle police headquarters for questioning about the 1957 kidnapping and murder of Maria Ridulph.

Jack automatically took the defensive position, claiming, "Maria was loved in the neighborhood, and was as sweet as could be, and she hardly said a word to anybody and everyone loved her." The state's attorney, Clay Campbell, felt that Jack was describing somebody that he was obsessed with and had thought a lot about.

The most damning part of the interrogation was when Jack came up with who he thought was the culprit. This raised a red flag for the cold case unit detectives who helped in the interview, as it was a classic answer by other serial killers that they had interviewed before, that they would help the detectives find the real murderer.

Jack told the investigators that the suspect just looked like him but wasn't. This also made the detectives think that he was trying to deflect their attention off of him. Jack would also tell the detectives about where he was on the night of the murder, and that he had an alibi. He was in Rockford, which is 40 miles away from Sycamore, being interviewed in an Army induction center.

The interrogation started with Jack standing with his face down, his hands cuffed behind his back, while he waited for the detectives to enter the interview room. As soon as the detectives entered the room, one of the officers started to remove the handcuffs from Jack's wrists. The other officer asked Jack if he could remove anything from his pockets, remove his jacket, and let them check his slippers. They then warned Jack that everything was going to be recorded, and let him use the restroom.

Jack McCullough in the Seattle interrogation room

After Jack returned to the interview room, another officer entered and asked Jack if he smoked and if he took any medication. Jack informed the officer that he took a lot of medication, as he was a heart patient.

Then entered Seattle homicide cold case Det. Michael Ciesynski, who asked Jack if he wanted a coffee and how many sugars he took in his coffee. It was a quick minute before he came back with the coffee for Jack.

A few minutes later, detectives Dave Alaskey and Brion Hanley of the Illinois State Police came into the room. Both introduced themselves to Jack and took a seat. Hanley sat directly across from Jack, and Alaskey took a seat off to the side of the room.

Hanley started out the interview, saying, "You probably remember a long time ago, 50 years ago, a young girl was abducted."

Jack interrupted the detective, saying, "I wrote, yeah, I called that in, I called the FBI about that."

Alaskey then started to review the case, saying, "Back on December 3, 1957—"

Jack interrupted, "Maria ...," and Alaskey replied, "Maria, exactly, and we've been going through and doing some new interviewing and new investigations regarding that, you know, regarding that weekend, you know, and I wanted to talk with you because there's, you know, there's a number of things that come, that came up you know, and additionally we value your insights in this. I know we kind of inconvenienced you, but I think we can come and get your help to, to resolve this."

"Yeah, yeah," Jack replied.

The detectives wanted to take care of the administrative items first by getting Jack's proper name, address, phone number, place of birth, etc. They wanted to know about any scars or tattoos that Jack had. The detectives soon asked about Jack's employer at the time, during which he was a security guard. The next thing the detectives wanted to review was if Jack were married now, and how many times that he was married before. Seeming to be irritated, Jack asked "You're investigating a child, right? You're not investigating me!" A detective quickly tried to calm Jack by telling him that this was only a personal history form that they fill out for everybody, as their command wants it. "I just do what I'm told," the detective said, while chuckling.

"After completing the documents of Jack's personal history, the detective told Jack that he had to do one more thing— and it didn't matter if Jack were a victim, witness, or suspect: read him his Miranda rights. Afterward, the detective asked if Jack understood his rights. Jack responded, "It's all good advice, but I'm on your side on this one. I'm trying to help you." The detectives reassured Jack that this was just a formality, and that they had to do this as it was the rule.

After a short pause, Jack went on to tell the detectives about a dream that he had, and how it reminded him of a conversation he had as a kid. "There's a little grade school, it's only a block away from my home in Sycamore which is 226, 227 Center Cross Street, and I was talking to a kid and he said you see that guy over there? And I was probably 13, oh when was that, oh, in 1957 I was 17, 18. Anyway, he said you see that kid, stay away from that kid, he wants to talk about sex." Jack broke away from his story and told the detectives that he'd have to reach back and remember his name and that he thought that he wrote it to the FBI. "Like my mom, it bothered me enough to where I called them," Jack continued, "and he lived with two boys named Davies, Don Davies is one of them, and I don't remember the other one. He was a kid that they allowed to stay with them. He didn't have a home in Sycamore. And it was on the same block as Maria lived."

Next, the detectives changed the subject and wanted to know about Sycamore and what kind of a place it was to live in. Jack compared it to Mayberry (the fictional town of a popular television series of the 1960s) and how you knew everybody who lived there. It would be a great place to raise children if they planned on having a family, Jack told the detectives. This was really small talk disguised to segue into Jack's family and his relationship with his sisters. When they asked him the ages and names of each of his sisters, Jack seemed to have a real problem remembering how old they were in comparison to himself. The detectives then wanted to know what they were like to grow up with, and Jack responded, "Great!," and went back to saying it was just like Mayberry or "Leave It to Beaver," and they all laughed.

You could hear the hesitation on the next question asked by the detective. "The, the, night Maria was kidnapped, tell me what you remember about that day Maria was kidnapped."

"I was in the induction center in Chicago." There was a long pause then, "Joining the Air Force. I spent the entire day there and they have a record of it minute by minute. I was really pissed off back then because the FBI even interrogated me because the suspect that took Maria had a green coat and I had a favorite green jacket at the time, so."

A portion of the interview is transcribed below:

Detective: "So how did you wind up at the induction center?"

Jack: "How I got there? I may have taken the train (short pause), but I was there most of the day and you can check with them because they gave me a lie detector test and I ... (a short pause) I was disappointed in them, really really disappointed because I had an iron-clad alibi of where I was and they didn't check, didn't even make a phone call! I was pretty disappointed."

D: "Well tell me about the day before, because you were going downtown or something, tell me as much as you can remember and as much detail as you can remember."

J: "You mean about downtown Chicago?"

D: "Yeah."

J: "Oh, it was a nightmare. The green machine there, have you ever been through there?"

D: "Downtown?"

J: "Yeah."

D: "Oh, sure."

J: "You've been through the induction center?"

D: "Oh, gosh, no."

J: "Oh, yeah, it was all day long and at the end of it, I got sworn in and it wasn't very long and I was on a train to Fort Knox."

D: "It seemed that in the file, you had a medical problem or something? There was a spot on the lungs or something."

J: "That was when I was a child, I had TB."

D: "According to the file, they saw a spot on your lung and they failed you, but then you had to stay and—"

J: "No, no, no, I passed because the scar was long gone by then. I mean the scar is still there, but I had good health."

D: "The report said that you had to stay downtown at the YMCA?"

J: "I don't remember that."

D: "What do you remember?"

Throughout the next while, the detectives pressured Jack to remember how he got downtown, but he just repeated that he must have taken the train. Jack got upset because they were treating him like a suspect again and told them that he didn't like it.

The detective told Jack that the story he had told the FBI back then doesn't match with what he was saying now. Jack, obviously irritated by now started to argue with the detectives. One of the detectives asked Jack what he did later that night and why he wasn't home. Jack told them he was home, and the detective then told Jack that his sisters said he wasn't home. They argued back and forth a few times until Jack blurted out, "Okay, we're done!"

After coaxing from detectives, Jack was persuaded to continue to talk, with a detective saying his memory might be jogged by reading the 1957 FBI report. After reading out some of what Jack had told the FBI, Jack said that he didn't remember any of that. Throughout the next while, as the officer read from the FBI report what Jack had said in 1957, he would keep saying that he didn't remember any of that and didn't know why he would say anything that the detective claimed he said.

Jack had told the FBI in 1957 that he got home about 10:30 p.m. the night Maria was kidnapped, and had helped search for her, which was the first thing that he remembered doing. He said he remembered searching some farms in DeKalb, but couldn't remember how he got to the farms. Jack couldn't remember if he went with anybody, but said that there were lots of people searching and he just joined them there that night.

The detective moved on to the description of the suspect, how it matched Jack according to the only witness, Kathy Sigmund, and how the suspect had worn a multi-colored sweater. Jack told them that he never had a multi-colored sweater, that he only wore his favorite green jacket back then. The detectives shocked Jack then by telling him that his sisters told them that Jack had a multi-colored sweater, which had gone missing after Maria was kidnapped. Jack's response was, "That's bullshit."

The next item for the detective was that Jack called his house on the evening of Maria's disappearance to get somebody to pick him up. The sisters had told police that their father couldn't pick up Jack as he was out taking Kathy to her club meeting and didn't get back until after 8:30, and the police had already arrived to help search for Maria. Jack later told the FBI that his father had picked him up at about 8 p.m. and that he was home by 9:20 p.m. to go out on a date with Jan.

Now, the police told Jack that Jan said that she didn't go out on a date with Jack that night. Jack then went back to claiming he didn't remember any of this.

It was at this point that the detective decided to bring up another discrepancy between Jack's story and what they had learned from his sisters about that night. Jack had told the FBI that once he finished helping to search for Maria, he had gone home and went to bed. His sisters, however, had told the FBI that Jack wasn't home that night and couldn't have come home, as when their parents had gone out to help search for Maria, they had put a lock on the front door so that nobody could get in and had put up 2 x 4s across the back entrance as they were scared. Their father had told the girls that one of them would have to sleep on the couch so that they could let their parents in when they got back home. The parents got home between 4 and 5 in the morning, and Jack wasn't there.

"So how does that make me a suspect?" Jack asked. "This is all bullshit, and I can't remember anything that I told them. Sounds to me like they're making shit up, and I already told you about how disappointed I am with the FBI!"

Detective: "You also told the FBI that you had some sex play with your sister."

Jack: "Oh, my God, I took a lie detector test!"

D: "We're talking about what you said, did you have sex with your sister? He asked when this was, and you said, 'When we were little,' and your sister said that this wasn't just when we were little."

J: "So? I'm telling you I don't remember any of this."

D: "Your mother also said to Janet and Mary that you killed her, Maria."

J: "This is a lie. It's a lie. My mother loved me to death. And she was crying when the FBI wanted to talk to me."

D: "I have no doubt, and she also told them some lies, to the FBI."

J: "My mother doesn't lie."

D: "Well, she said you were home all night. And the girls said, 'He couldn't be in. We looked he wasn't home. The doors were locked and nobody could get in without us opening the door.' And your mother didn't tell the truth and she may have been protecting you."

J: "You mean by saying that I murdered a girl? This is all bullshit. My mother wouldn't say that. My mother knew where I was that day."

D: "I absolutely agree with you that you were down in the city that day having a physical. It's irrelevant where you were that day; that means nothing. Because the incident doesn't happen until 6 o'clock at night."

J: "And where was I?"

D: "You claim in Rockford."

J: "So? If I'm in Rockford at 7 o'clock and make a phone call from there and ask for a ride—"

D: "But nobody can come get you."

J: "So? I've got a thumb and I can hitchhike."

The detective brought up another issue with Jack's story. The military office gave Jack a ticket for the train so that he could go to Rockford, but he never used the ticket. The police were given the ticket from Jack's girlfriend at the time, Jan, who told them that Jack had given it to her back then, and she kept it.

J: "I'm not involved in any of this and I'll take a lie detector test and I'll pass, okay!"

D: "Okay, why don't we do that right now."

J: "Okay."

D: "We will be back in just a sec."

J (to one detective): "I want to talk to you."

D: "You want to talk to me?"

J: "Yeah."

D: "About what?"

J: "About what, who I think did it."

D: "Okay."

The detective sat down and the other detective left the interrogation room.

J: "Nobody seems to be interested in what I'm saying."

D: "Okay."

J: "I may have to contact you again when I come up with the name because it's in here (Jack points to his head)."

D: "I'll give you my business card."

J: "Okay, but this kid that lived with the Davies. The Davies lived on the same side of the street as Maria. They live right across the street from this little grade school. And I'm trying to remember ... Anyway, years later it dawned on me, this guy would have been perfect. He would have been about my height. He looked something like me."

D: "You said what was his name?"

J: "I'm trying to think of it."

D: "It's not coming to you?"

J: "It's not coming to me, but when I called the FBI, I gave them his name."

D: "So, they should have it?"

J: "They should have it. Anyway, this guy did look something like me, and I don't know if he had a gap in his teeth, but he was weird."

D: "How do you know that?"

J: "This kid told me and I observed."

D: "Okay, so you don't know that firsthand. Like what's weird?"

J: "Not normal."

D: "You observed this? Or this is what that other boy said?"

J: "I observed it. I'd seen him around the neighborhood a few times and I didn't like him, so I didn't have any kind of relationship with him or conversation with him. But I remember him that day on the school ground and one of the kids telling me if I knew him, and I said I knew him and he wasn't standing very far from me and he said he talks about sex, little kids stuff you know, so stay away from him. So, I just recorded that and forgot it until years later."

D: "Mm-hmm, but you understand the inconsistencies and whatnot."

J: "You can find anything from anything, but I was devastated when that little girl was taken."

D: "Would there be a reason why your mom would say something like that?"

J: "There is no reason my mom would say that. I don't believe that was said. My mother loved me."

D: "You guys were close?"

J: "Very close."

D: "You loved her."

J: "Absolutely."

D: "She loved you. Why do you think she would say something like that?"

J: "She didn't say something like that. She wouldn't say something like that. It's a lie."

D: "Who is lying?"

J: "Whoever said that."

D: "You don't talk to your brothers and sisters now?"

J: "No."

D: "Why, I mean your brothers and sisters?"

J: "We've just grown apart."

D: "Why did you move to Seattle?"

J: "I was in the military here."

D: "You didn't want to move back to Sycamore?"

J: "God, no."

D: "Why? It's Mayberry."

J: "Take a look around. How many mountains you got in Illinois? You got one hill, and we got everything here. We got wonderful, beautiful weather. We got the mountains. We got the trees."

D: "Let me ask you this. You said that when you were younger you had a sexual encounter with your sister— accidentally, on purpose, doesn't matter. That was the only time that that happened? Jack, be honest with me."

J: "I don't know."

D: "You don't know if that was the only time?"

J: "No."

D: "So, there could have been other times, when you got older?"

J: "Yeah, but this doesn't make me a suspect in a murder!"

D: "Did I say that? No."

J: "Then why are you asking?"

D: "It's just information that we have gotten and when Dave asked you if you had sex with your sisters more than once, you said no, and that's a lie."

J: "I never had sex."

D: "What did you have?

J: "Just playing around."

D: "Okay, so just playing around with your sister."

J: "Yeah."

D: "We just want you to be honest."

J: "What has this got to do with this little girl?"

D: "The questions that we ask you, we know the answers."

J: "You think you know the answers. Let me tell you something, I did not kidnap that little girl!"

D: "Listen, we're going to take a little break, and I'll give you my business card."

J: "Yeah, and I'll call you as soon as I remember that name."

D: "Okay, you call me."

J: "That's who you should be looking at."

D: "We can't until you give us the name."

J: "I already gave you the name Don Davies. You ask him who that guy was that lived with them."

D: "So, Don Davies wasn't the strange guy?"

J: "No, he was the tough guy, every one was afraid of him because he was tough. I can't remember the name now, but I did when I called and gave it to the FBI."

After a restroom break, Jack returned to the room alone. As soon as Jack sat down, he turned, looked into the two-way mirror, said that he remembered the name and asked the detective to come back into the room. He said, "You're recording this, so his name is Brooks."

The detective came into the room and asked Jack what the name was again, and he replied that it was "Brooks."

Detective: "'Do you remember his first name, or was that his first name?"

Jack: "No, that was his last name. I don't remember his first name."

D: "So, can I ask you when you were talking about messing around with …"

J: "No, we're not talking about that. We're done. You follow up on Brooks."

The detective left and Jack was taken for a polygraph test. After the test, he was brought back into the interview room by an officer. Jack sat down and asked, "Are we done? Or are you going to arrest me?"

Officer: "You'll have to see what the detectives say. I think they're going to come in and ask you some more questions."

The officer left the room.

It was a while later when the two detectives came back into the room and told Jack that the polygraph didn't go so well for him.

Jack: "So, are you guys going to arrest me or what?"

Detective one: "To be honest with you, we haven't quite decided that. I still have some issues with this. I appreciate the fact that we are talking a long time ago, and if we can come up with an alternative ..."

J: "You ain't got shit or you would have arrested me."

Detective one: "Is he free to go?"

Detective two: "No."

Jack: "Did you say no?"

Detective one: "Yes, we will come back and let you know what the arrangements for tonight will be."

A few minutes later, Jack asked to use the bathroom again. On his way back into the room, he asked the officer if someone could come in and tell him if they were going to arrest him.

Soon Ciesynski from the Seattle Police Department cold case unit returned to the interview room to talk with Jack. Michael explained how he was a cold case detective for the Seattle Police Department and that he was assisting the Illinois State Police with the case.

Ciesynski: "Things not go to well on the polygraph, I take it?"

Jack: "No. No, she (referring to the polygraph examiner) was fishing, and I'm anxious for this case to be solved. We're talking about the murder of a little girl. But she's fishing in my personal life. I ain't answering any questions like that."

C: "Well, your personal life is what's at issue right now."

J: "No, the little girl is."

C: "Correct."

J: "Does anything make me a murderer, I'm not! Why would I call the FBI with a name that came to me in the middle of the night if I—"

C: "What name was that?"

J: "I hope to hell they look at it! Don Davies and Ken Davies and, umm, Brooks! Brooks looks really, um—"

C: "The information from back then, the Illinois State Police—"

J: "Did they talk to him?"

Ciesynski then nodded yes and muttered, um-hum while he took a drink of his coffee.

J: "They did! Well, that's my best shot."

C: "That actually was pretty good information. Some of this was inconclusive, and as you know, there was a whole list of suspects at the time of this case. All I do is work cold case homicides. I'm in this room all the time dealing with guys from your age to mid-50s. I work cases from the late 1950s and usually up into the 1990s. That's all I ever do, so I know what this is all about, and I know guys in your position also. I can usually tell when somebody is lying to me, whether they got something to hide or they have some reasons why they might be lying, and because a lot of times, it's embarrassing about certain aspects of their life. Like I know some of the issues that are embarrassing to you and with your family. I don't give a shit about that. There's nothing really to do with this case, okay! I realize that I'm not going to ask you about you and your sisters, things happened like that and it has nothing to do with this case. Okay?"

J: "Yeah, yeah."

C: "One of the problems that I have here in reviewing this case, everyone like in your position and stuff, there's a reason why they want to hide a little bit of something. If there's some type of embarrassment, even back then, when you want to contact the FBI and help them out, which you did. I also believe that you helped with the search, too, I believe?"

J: "I did!"

C: "You actually know the area pretty well. You even knew the area down below in the later facts."

J: "Okay, I didn't know where she was kept, where she was recovered."

C: "You don't know where she was recovered at?"

J: "No."

C: "What was the name of that area?"

J: "How could I know if I don't know?!"

C: "Well, I mean, it was in the newspapers and you lived around there."

J: "All I know, and this is a vague recollection, it was somewhere wooded, it was south of town, I think, and it was quite a distance."

C: "Quite a distance from?"

J: "Sycamore."

C: "Okay."

J: "And that I'm getting from the newspaper, and the people who found her were supposedly mushroom hunting, but the article said that they didn't believe their story because it wasn't mushroom season."

C: "Okay, mushroom season usually comes in spring, from early spring until late spring, I believe, looking at my grass sometimes, but I believe she was found in April, right?"

J: "I don't know. I was in the service then."

C: "When she was found, you were in the service?"

J: "Yes."

C: "You said she was found far away from home. I heard she was found in another county somewhere, but how could she have gotten there?"

J: "I don't know, obviously."

C: "What mode of transportation could they have had?"

J: "They had to have had a car."

C: "A car or truck, something like that, because it was that type of distance and this was I believe like December 3. Do you know what the weather was like?"

J: "It was 50 years ago! Come on!"

C: "Yeah, but you were out there searching for her and I don't remember it."

J: "There was snow."

C: "You mentioned a couple of names, Davies—"

J: "Davies and Brooks. He lived with Don and Ken."

C: "They were your friends?"

J: "No, they were neighbors and ruffian neighbors."

C: "Associates?"

J: "No, no, I did not have anything to do with them, didn't have any contact with them at all."

C: "You never hung out with these guys?"

J: "No, these guys were bad."

C: "Oh, okay."

J: "Don turned out okay. I don't know how Ken turned out, but Don got married and last I saw of him he had a painting business. He painted houses and he was a tough guy. Personally, I would be afraid of him."

C: "You and him ever mix it up at all?"

J: "No! No! Are you kidding?"

C: "You were in pretty good shape back then."

J: "He was older and I didn't have any contact with him at all. The only thing that I ever had contact with him, I beat Kevin one time wrestling."

C: "Okay."

J: "But that's just neighborhood stuff. I probably only had two contacts with the older one in my whole life."

C: "So, you were leery of these guys? You would never go and rat these guys out and have it come back on you?"

J: "No, I don't suspect them of anything."

C: "You don't suspect them of anything? Not even in this case you don't speculate—"

J: "No, no."

C: "But didn't you give the FBI their names?"

J: "I didn't give them Kevin and Don's names, Brooks."

C: "Okay, Brooks."

J: "I just woke up out of a sound sleep and thought, 'Yes, that's him. He did it, because—' "

C: "Where were you when this happened? Were you in your army barracks?"

J: "No, this was last year. I think it was last year? Maybe it was earlier. Anyway, it was when I called the FBI, which was in the last few months. I felt so strongly about it I called them up and left a message and they never got back to me."

C: "This little girl that was murdered here, you were a good guy back in the day, and this was a neighbor girl and you were a tight-knit community, and there were two girls there, but they didn't really know you, right? Obviously, they're not going to know an 18-year-old man. I mean, they're little girls."

J: "No, I recognize the little girl. I knew her name."

C: "Oh, okay."

J: "And she was, if you were on her block, she never wandered very far from her home?"

C: "I want to tell you exactly how I feel. I feel that you're hiding something, that you're holding something back, and you did something that's embarrassing you. You got to realize that you're kind of in a world of shit right now, okay, and you're going to have to give up the truth okay, to save your own ass, to be smart, okay? Just listen to me. That's all I'm asking, all right? There's certain things that happened here, right, that I know happened, that you know happened here. I'm not saying from reviewing this file, I'm not saying that you killed this girl."

J: "I did not!"

C: "I'm not saying you did, that's what I'm investigating. You're holding back some things here."

J: "Which has nothing to do with anything, okay!"

C: "That's the part you're going to have to get out and let me decide, okay?"

J: "If we turn away from the little girl's murder—"

C: "I don't want to go away from the little girl's murder. You're worried about something else, but that's not the point. You're missing my point. I'm talking about the little girl's murder here, that you're holding something back. I believe from all of the reports I read, that the other little girl who was there—"

J: "But I don't know, what 'other little girl'?"

C: "There were two little girls there. There were two little girls out there, and they were playing out there, when I believe that you came up there."

J: "What!"

C: "Now listen, I'm not saying that you killed that girl, do you understand me?"

J: "Oh, man!"

C: "That's what I believe happened. You read the newspaper reports, and did you Google this stuff at all when you called the FBI?"

J: "No."

C: "Because I went to your house and noticed you had a computer there, you did no research on this at all?"

J: "No. No!"

C: "Did your wife do any research on this?"

J: "NO!"

C: "Did you ever look it up in the Sycamore Times or newspapers?"

J: "No."

C: "Okay, but you made some reference to reading newspapers before, though?"

J: "Correct. The only information that I got out of the Sycamore newspaper I gave you before."

C: "When was that? At the time or recently?"

J: "Recently."

C: "So, there wasn't just one girl there, there were two. They were best friends."

J: "Really?"

C: "Yes, she is still alive today and actually got interviewed by two detectives here. And once again, this is where I believe that you are hiding something, and I'll tell you why I think you're hiding something."

J: "I'm going to tell you where you're wrong."

C: "Okay, but you better hear what I say first before you say I'm wrong, okay?"

J: "Yeah."

C: "What I believe happened here is that you did go up there. These two girls were up there, and they knew the guy's name was Johnny. Johnny said, and he was really nice to the girl, he knew Maria, and he offered them a piggyback ride. And I believe that that person was you and—"

J: "Oh, my God!"

C: "—and that you did give them a piggyback ride."

J: "All right, I'm lawyering up!"

C: "Just listen to what I'm saying. You did give them a piggyback ride, but I'm not saying that you killed her."

J: "There is no way I could have even been in the area, okay? I was in the induction center all day long. I didn't even, when she got, what time of day she got, I found out when I got home. Mom says that Maria's been kidnapped, okay? That's all I know. But I made a phone call from Rockford, which you got, at 7 o'clock after I got off the train. Sycamore is 30 miles away from Rockford. This is an hour after she was kidnapped. I was on the train."

C: "So, you took the train there?"

J: "From Chicago to Rockford."

C: "From Chicago to Rockford."

J: "Yeah."

C: "Now, why would you end up in Chicago?"

J: "Chicago is where the induction center was."

C: "That's where the AFIT station is in Chicago?"

J: "Yeah, yeah, I spent the whole damn day there and they got records, they had records of me from every goddamn minute that I arrived. I mean, they were looking at my butt and everything. All day long, and when I was done with it, I don't remember perfectly, but I'm assuming that I took the train, because I wouldn't drive my car to Chicago, and I got rid of my car anyway because I was going into the service."

C: "But you did have your car at that time, though?"

J: "No."

C: "I believe it was a DeSoto?"

J: "No, a '48 Plymouth Coupe piece of crap."

C: "You say that you had got rid of that car already?"

J: "Yeah, yeah."

C: "So, somebody took you to the train station?"

J: "Yeah, yeah."

C: "And that was your friend, or...?"

J: "I don't know."

C: "You just don't remember?"

J: "Yeah."

C: "Okay, and so the Air Force gave you a ticket to come to Chicago or Rockford? I don't remember."

J: "I was in Chicago at the induction center."

C: "So how did you get to Chicago?"

J: "I don't remember. I probably took the train, but this is 50 years ago and I don't know."

C: "I'm going to go grab you a picture, just sit right here, all right?"

J: "All right."

Ciesynski left the room. Five minutes later when the detective came back into the room, he sat down and presented a file folder with pictures inside.

C: "Detectives from the Illinois State Police, the ones who initiated this investigation, the FBI did it back when I believe that you talked to them?"

J: "Yes, yes, I took a lie detector and I passed it!"

C: "Actually, I looked at that lie detector also. Did they tell you that you passed it?"

J: "They freed me!"

C: "Did they tell you that you passed it?"

J: "I don't recall. The agent that I talked to just took me home. I volunteered to go. I didn't have to go and they took me up to a motel on DeKalb Highway and that's where they conducted the thing. And they played Mutt and Jeff, one guy was mean to me the other guy was like you, the good guy. The bad cop was like, yelling, 'I know you did it!' "

C: "He was playing the bad cop? We don't really use that much. Most of them here were trying to get the truth out of you."

J: "Yeah, yeah. Are you going to show me a picture?"

C: "Yeah, and I'm going to ask you about somebody else also. Do you know a guy named Dennis, Dennis?"

J: "It doesn't ring a bell."

C: "Is it Trudell?"

J: "Trudell, yes, yes."

C: "What you do know about Dennis?"

J: "I lost track of him because he got married young."

C: "And?"

J: "That was all."

C: "Your relationship, you had a pretty close-knit family. Your mom is deceased now?"

J: "Yeah."

C: "You were real tight with her?"

J: "Oh, absolutely. I called my mom every month of my life. I loved my mom and my mom was brilliant. When she died, my dad was asked how many people he thought were gonna come to the funeral and dad says maybe 30 to 40, but 350 people showed up."

C: "Did you show up?"

J: "No, I was in the service."

C: "They wouldn't let you go home from the military for your mom's funeral? Were you in Vietnam then?"

J: "I don't remember where I was."

C: "When did your mom die?"

J: "I don't remember the year. Oh, let me see, I was here. I was here. I did go home to see her one last time, but I didn't go to the funeral."

C: "Was there a falling out or something?"

J: "No."

C: "No problem with your sisters?"

J: "No, it was just how things worked out."

C: "Who's the next oldest? You're the oldest, right?"

J: "Yeah."

C: "Who is the next oldest sibling?"

J: "Kathy."

C: "Did Kathy ever talk to you about this? In later years after your mom passed away?"

J: "No."

C: "She's never mentioned to you about this case at all?"

J: "No."

C: "Did your mom ever talk to you about this case at all?"

J: "No, no."

C: "Even, I'm talking way back, you know, at the time."

J: "The only thing Mom talked about was when I was going to go to see the FBI, she was crying, and I said, 'Mom, don't worry about it.' "

C: "So, you did talk to your mother about it and she was worried about it?"

J: "Sure, sure."

C: "And you just went down there and took the polygraph and you came back home and told your mother that you passed the polygraph?"

J: "Yeah."

C: "I'm going to lay out a couple of things for you. Why do you think this case got reopened?"

J: "Probably because I made the call to the FBI."

C: "Which field office did you call?"

J: "New York."

C: "You called the New York FBI office from Seattle?"

J: "I think so, let me think. One time I called the local FBI office."

C: "By local, you mean Seattle?"

J: "Seattle, yes."

C: "Would you call from your cell phone?"

J: "No, I called from home."

C: "From your house here?"

J: "Yeah."

C: "And the agent never called you back?"

J: "No."

C: "So, were you able to talk to an agent?"

J: "No, wait a minute. When I called the Seattle office, it was about something else. A friend of mine, who was Pakistani, told me something about some stuff going on in the mosque. So, I called up the FBI and told them that they were trash talking us in the mosque and the person that I talked to said, 'Don't worry about it, we got the mosque covered.' So that's the only time that I talked to the FBI here. I'm pretty sure that I talked to the FBI in New York.

C: "In New York, and this was about this case? And you were inquiring about what the status was in the case?"

J: "No, I told them about the guy, the guy, tell me the name ..."

C: "Of the guy we just mentioned?"

J: "Yeah, yeah, yeah, Brooks."

C: "Oh, about Brooks?"

J: "Yeah."

C: "Why didn't you call the Chicago field office? I'm just curious."

J: "I just don't know."

The detective then opened up his file and started to lay out the pictures that he had onto the table. He said, "Remember earlier I told you that I didn't think that you killed her?"

J: "Yeah."

C: "Let me show you something. I said that I believe that you were there, and there was the other little girl that was there. Now, I'm not saying that you were there when she was killed, I'm not saying that. I'm not saying that you took the girl."

As Jack started to tell the detective that he was absolutely wrong, the detective finished laying out the row of six pictures face up on the table. Just as he finished, Jack said, "I don't know any of them."

C: "All right. Remember I told you that there were two little girls there? And the one girl, she got killed, and the other girl said that the person who came there who said his name was Johnny and he lived nearby and gave them a piggyback ride. He was very nice, and she said he was one of these guys here. Can you picture anybody out here that you know?"

J: "I don't know any of these guys and I don't think any of these guys are from Sycamore."

C: "Can you take a look at each of these pictures?"

A long pause occurred as Jack went through each picture, appearing to take his time looking at the faces, and after each picture he would just say no.

J: "These guys ain't from Sycamore."

The detective picked up the third photo and asked Jack who he thought the guy looked like. Jack took another minute then answered, "I don't know." Another pause, then Jack looked back at the detective and said, "It might look like me. But he's too feminine-looking."

The detective told Jack that it was a picture of Jack from a wedding picture. It was a copy of a wedding photo of Jack and had been put into a montage shown to the surviving girl, who said it was Johnny, the guy who gave the girls a piggyback ride.

C: "They didn't say you killed her, but that's what they're saying. Now, from all of the information that we have, do you want to know who else said that you did it? It's from someone who I read is a very smart person, a very intelligent person, someone who lived with a lot of guilt for a long time before she passed away and—"

J: "You're gonna say my mom, that's bullshit!"

C: "Why do you say that's bullshit?"

J: "Because she wouldn't suspect me of murdering and she knew where I was."

C: "I'm telling you exactly. I'm sorry. The documentation said she said that you're the one who did this, and she was ashamed of it. And the little girl that saw Johnny signed the back of your photo saying that you did it. Now, Jack, I still think that you're covering for somebody. I think somebody did something there, and you were there when this girl got killed. You were there when the girl got the piggyback ride. I'm not saying that you took the girl who got killed, I'm saying you were there and then you walked off and somebody else came up to her and you remember this, and you're trying to hide it or cover for somebody. I don't know who your trying to cover for, but—"

J: "I'm not covering for anybody! And I don't know what you're talking about. I don't think that I ever gave Maria or her friends any piggyback ride for Christ sakes!"

C: "Oh, it's Maria, not the other girl, the other girl was standing there and she saw you and she completely picked you out, and now there's no doubt in my mind that you were the person that was there. Not saying you were the one who killed her. You're trying to hide something else. I don't know if you're trying to cover for somebody or what, but you were the person that was there during this time."

J: "This is two blocks away from my house. Everybody in the neighborhood knows me."

C: "What did they know you as? Did they know you as Johnny?"

J: "Yeah. Well, there were two Johnnys. I was big Johnny, and he was little Johnny, the other kid was little Johnny."

C: "Who was the other kid?"

J: "Johnny Boies, he lived one house away."

C: "Was he with you?"

J: "No."

C: "Did you hang with the guy?"

J: "No. He was younger than me. They called him Butterball as well. His brother's name was Ed, and he was John as well, so all the neighbors would call me big John."

C: "Well, she said that this is the Johnny who did it. She didn't say that you hurt anybody. But she's saying that you were the guy there that gave them the piggyback ride. She went back home to go get a doll or go get mittens, and when she came back, the two of you were gone. So, it's either saying that you actually left that area and the little girl left with somebody else, okay. But there's no doubt in my mind that you were the guy that was there. Now, you got to tell us exactly what happened there, okay? And by saying that you don't remember this, you do remember this, because you remember so many details about that day."

J: "You're full of shit, okay? I don't remember anything like this!"

C: "You don't remember anything at all? Do you remember giving any little girl a piggyback ride?"

J: "No."

C: "Have you ever given her a piggyback ride?"

J: "No."

C: "Neither one of the girls?"

J: "Neither one of them."

C: "You never gave neighbors or your sisters a piggyback ride? You were good with kids in the neighborhood, weren't you?"

J: "The last time I saw her was probably months before this happened. She was just walking down the street, I just passed her and that's the last I saw her."

C: "Was she by herself?"

J: "Yeah."

C: "So, this was months before, so this had to be in October or something? Did she say, 'Hi, Johnny'?"

J: "She didn't know me."

C: "So, she didn't know you?"

J: "Yeah."

C: "And so, she walked by your house?"

J: "No, she wouldn't walk more than a block, she wouldn't walk more than two or three houses away from her house. She was just little."

C: "How would you know that? You're just surmising."

J: "I've seen, I lived in the neighborhood. You know, the neighborhood boys and me would play, and we would see the other kids playing."

C: "It was just a normal neighborhood. Now, the other guys, you said with the girls around, and the other guys you would hang out with and stuff, and you're young, 17 or 18 years old at the time?"

J: "I was 17, I guess, and I went in the Air Force the day after ... yeah, I think I just turned 18 after I got in the service."

C: "And you seen these guys around the neighborhood just sitting around on the stoop or, you know, sitting on the porch, in the neighborhoods like we used to do back in the days?"

J: "Right, right."

C: "Guys sitting around, sometimes they might say something a little raunchy or something, usually towards older girls. But did you have any suspicions about these other guys?"

J: "No."

C: "None of these guys that you hung out with?"

J: "NO. As a matter of fact, they're all, one of them is a banker, the other one I think is a lawyer."

They both laughed at that comment.

C: "I'm just saying, as you also mentioned some of the guys that you were afraid of, right?"

J: "Yeah."

C: "The Davies boys. So, this little girl just came walking by. Did you know her family?"

J: "I knew her family and her sisters. But I didn't know the family. I had seen them and I had been over—"

Just then, Jack stood up quickly and screamed out, "Oh, my God!" He grabbed the back of his leg up near his buttocks and started rubbing it. The detective offered him some water, but he refused. Jack remained standing, rubbed the top part of his right leg and continued to explain.

J: "I had been over to their house a couple of times. Her sisters were aspiring actresses and so they would always create a play or something like that. One time, I was invited back there to watch one of their plays, and that was the one time that I went over."

C: "Did you ever handle her jacket or clothing or anything like that?"

J: "I never touched anything."

C: "You never touched her jacket? When you were at her house?"

J: "I never touched anything."

C: "Your sisters, were they about the same age as her sisters?"

J: "They didn't play over there with those people."

C: "How did you get hooked up with these people?"

J: "The sisters, the older ones, there were two sisters, one was about my age. I'm just, I don't know."

Then Jack began to rub his leg, stand and sit, and seemed really restless at this point.

J: "Patty was the oldest one, and she would put on a play."

C: "So, you would go over there and see the plays and stuff."

J: "I went one time."

C: "But they invited you other times, you said?"

J: "No."

C: "Oh, they only invited you one time?"

J: "One time."

C: "And you went there to watch the play?"

J: "Yeah, which I didn't think much of."

C: "It wasn't much of a—"

J: "Yeah."

C: "Sit right there. I have something."

The detective left the room. After the detective left, Jack stood up and moved his chair away from the area that he was standing in, then started to bend over and touch his toes with his fingers. I think he was trying to stretch out so that the pain that he was getting in his upper thigh would stop.

When the detective came back into the room, he threw a picture onto the table in front of Jack and asked, "Who is that?"

J: "Oh, that's me."

The detective took a seat and then placed another picture on the table.

C: "That's you, too."

J: "This is a very poor picture of me. I can hardly recognize myself."

The detective leaned back into his chair and said nothing, then threw another picture onto the table. The detective broke the silence.

C: "You remember that night?"

J: "No."

A long pause ensued and Jack stood up, leaving his hands on the table, keeping his eyes on the picture, and said, "No," again. There was another long pause, and then Jack continued. "I was in love with that woman for so many years and she didn't even know it." Another long pause filled the room. The detective sat up in his chair, leaned forward, and began to look at the picture as well. The detective asked what the date was on the picture.

J: "1957, June 22."

Jack continued to stand and stare at the picture. "Thank you for showing me this. This brings back wonderful memories."

The detective sat back up in his chair and grabbed the picture, flipped it over, and pointed at the back of the picture. He then sat back in his chair and waited. After a few minutes of silence, Jack said, "I don't even remember this at all." Then Jack flipped over the picture and continued to look at it.

C: "That's Jan, correct?" (Referring to Jack's girlfriend back at the time of the kidnapping in 1957)

J: "Yeah, Janice."

C: "Do you remember you said a couple times that you took the FBI polygraph test?"

J: "Yeah."

C: "And you told your mother that you passed it?"

J: "Yeah."

C: "I want you to know, you failed that test. Did the FBI tell you that you passed the test?"

J: "I watched the test. I was hooked up to it. I watched the test. It didn't have any—"

Shwoo schwoo noises came out of Jack's mouth as he waved both hands back and forth as to be saying "no."

C: "Did they ask you if you murdered her?"

J: "Um, 'did you kill her?' I guess."

C: "There were questions on the polygraph back then that showed that you were deceptive, like when they asked if you knew anything about the girl's disappearance, or if you had seen the two girls there that night, it was deceptive once again. Then, when I asked you earlier if you had ever given the girls a piggyback ride and you said you might have—"

J: "Never! Remember me asking you for a lawyer? As we were walking out of the building, I said I want a lawyer, and you were standing right beside me."

C: "Who did you say that to?"

J: "You."

C: "You said that to me?"

J: "Yes."

C: "In this building here?"

J: "No, up at my building."

C: "At the Four Freedoms?"

J: "Yeah."

C: "No, I don't recall that."

J: "Because you said, 'Don't worry about it.' "

C: "That's what I said? When we were driving here?"

J: "No, when we were walking out of the building."

C: "So, what is it that you're saying to me now?"

J: "What I'm saying to you now, is that you think I had something to do with this."

C: "When did I tell you I think you got something to do with the murder? The thing that I think you had something to do with is you being there with those two girls before she was taken. I said you're being deceptive about something. You were deceptive in your polygraph with the FBI, you were deceptive when your mother on her deathbed believes you were involved in this, on her deathbed she said this. Are you telling me that you don't know about that?"

J: "I don't believe that."

C: "You don't believe that?"

J: "No."

C: "I'm going to find the documentation on that and I'm going to bring it to you."

J: "It doesn't matter."

C: "Why would your mother say that? In all the reports that I read, it doesn't seem like your mother's the type of person that's going to make something up out of nowhere."

J: "No, and this didn't happen."

C: "What didn't happen?"

J: "What you're telling me didn't happen."

C: "That your mother didn't say you did this on her deathbed?"

J: "Right, my mother knew I didn't do it."

C: "Yeah, so she just made this up?"

J: "Somebody made this up, there's a whole bunch of making up here!"

C: "Who's making up?"

J: "You said so many things today that I had no knowledge of."

C: "Well, I don't know what the other guys asked you about, but this girl here was saying that this was Johnny."

The detective moved the picture so it was in front of Jack. "This girl here gives us an unused train ticket that you were supposed to use that night." The detective then held up the picture of Jan, Jack's girlfriend at the time of the disappearance.

J: "There's no way that she (referring to his mother) would say any of this unless she was out of her mind. She died of cancer. They took so much out of her that there wasn't anything left."

C: "She never mentioned this to you at the end?"

J: "No."

The detective took a drink of water and passed a picture to Jack, then an officer came into the room and offered Jack some pizza, which he accepted. The detective left the room. Jack ate one piece of pizza and waited for the detective to return. After several minutes, the detective came into the room, noticed that Jack had only eaten one slice and asked if he wanted more pizza. Jack kind of shrugged and mumbled something to the detective.

J: "Now that I know that you think I had something to do with this, I want a lawyer."

C: "You do not want to talk to me, is that what you're saying?"

J: "Yeah, we're done."

C: "Yeah, that's fine with me, and you'll be booked."

J: "You heard of the fruit of a poisonous tree, right? Everything that you asked me since we left the building is no good, you know."

C: "Everything that I've asked you since we left the building?"

J: "Right. I asked for a lawyer."

C: "You asked me for a lawyer?"

J: "Yeah, I said I want a lawyer."

C: "And I said no?"

J: "No, you didn't say no, but you blew me off."

C: "I blew you off?"

J: "Yeah."

C: "You're going to be arrested. You're under arrest for murder."

J: "Okay."

C: "You're going to be placed into the King County Jail."

J: "Okay. Any phone calls?"

C: "The phone call stuff all comes from the jail. We haven't anything to do with that. You will have your first appearance tomorrow. You're going to be extradited. Even if you fight extradition, you're going to be extradited to Chicago. You will be placed in the DeKalb County jail."

J: "I am innocent! Prove it!"

C: "What did I say?"

J: "You've made up your mind."

C: "Did I say you killed that girl?"

J: "You've made up your mind already."

C: "Did I say that you killed that girl? No, I didn't say that to you. What did I say the only thing that you did?"

J: "Tell me."

C: "I'll tell you exactly what I said. I said I knew you were out there giving those girls a piggyback ride right? I didn't say you killed her."

J: "Between you and me, I want the person who did this."

C: "What do you want to happen to them?"

J: "I want the electric chair."

C: "They don't have that here in the state of Washington."

J: "We're done. Where's my lawyer?"

C: "You'll get it when you get to Illinois."

J: "Give me a call sometime. You think you're right, but you're not."

The detective then took Jack's watch and checked Jack's pockets to make sure they were empty.

REVIEW OF EVIDENCE

So, what do we have? First of all, we know that the two girls (Kathy Sigmund and Maria Ridulph) went out to play in the snow in the early evening of December 3, 1957. They were soon approached by a friendly man named "Johnny," who offered to give them piggyback rides. One of the girls (Kathy Sigmund) went into her house to grab a doll to show off to "Johnny" and when she returned, both Johnny and Maria were gone. The time was estimated between 6 and 7 p.m., as Kathy's father was watching his favorite western on television. Back in the fall of 1957, this show was on in Chicago at that time.

The police were called and there was a neighborhood all-out search that went on all night, and for many months to follow. Jack McCullough, known then as John, was in Chicago earlier that day applying to get into the military. Later on in the day, he ended up in the suburb of Rockford, where when he completed what he had to do for tests for the induction office. He called his mother at home and asked for his father to come and pick him up. We now know that the time of this phone call was 6:57 p.m.

Was it possible for Jack to have made it home and kidnap Maria?

The prosecutor, Clay Campbell, felt that Jack was home earlier, took Maria, then drove to Rockford and made the phone call. Campbell thought that this was Jack's way of setting up an alibi for himself. Campbell also said he had a witness to Jack's car being driven around in town that day, and because Jack couldn't remember how he got into Chicago and his train ticket was unused, he probably drove. Jack has claimed that he had already sold his car as he was planning on leaving town for military service.

Another issue that the prosecutor had was why hadn't Kathy been able to identify Jack?

Could it be possible that even though Jack only lived around the corner from Kathy, that they didn't know each other? Or they had never seen each other before, even though the town was only about 7,000 people and considered by all a very close-knit community, described as "Mayberry"? Kathy was shown many pictures, including photos of Jack, at the time of the kidnapping and did not identify him.

We also have to admit that Kathy was only an 8-year-old girl, and far too young to rely on as a witness. Kathy also gave several descriptions of "Johnny" and none of them were even close to what Jack looked like.

The other issue everyone was facing was the deathbed confession by Jack's mother, and that she had lied about the events of that evening. It was claimed that Jack's mother, who was sick with cancer at the time, in great pain and on heavy drugs such as morphine, had made such claims by Jack's two sisters, Janet and Mary. The two sisters also claim that Jack did not come home the night of the kidnapping, and their father never left to go pick up Jack in Rockford. But as Jack and his two sisters were not on speaking terms, and, in fact, the sisters hated Jack, could their testimony of what their mother told them when she was dying be believable?

Clay Campbell reviewed the evidence and realized that he really didn't have enough to get a conviction of Jack McCullough. So, he decided to go ahead and charge Jack with the rape of his sister, Jeanne Tessier. It's clear that if Campbell were able to prove Jack had raped his own sister, he would be able to take that forward in the Maria Ridulph murder case, which would help to seal Jack's fate.

The first thing Campbell did was go back through Jack's past to find out anything that he could to help taint Jack's credibility. In came a woman, once a teenage girl, who made claims against Jack when he was a policeman years before. Michelle Weinman.

MICHELLE WEINMAN

When Jack left the military, he had been a captain in the Air Force. He decided to move to the Seattle area. After graduating from the King County law enforcement academy in 1974, he got a job in Lacey, which neighbors Olympia, Washington. In Lacey, Jack married his second wife, Laura, whom he had met working a moonlighting job for Laura's father as a bodyguard. The marriage only lasted about three years, as Jack was caught cheating on Laura.

In 1979, Jack moved to Milton, near Tacoma, where he worked for the local police detachment, which was a much larger police department than Lacey. Now single, Jack was soon known as a lady's man. His new police chief, Harold Burton, thought of Jack as nothing but difficult. He fired Jack for tipping off a drug suspect, which Jack fought.

Burton said that the police station constantly received phone calls from bill collectors looking for Jack and also had several complaints from other employees about Jack's crude language and dirty jokes.

Burton wrote a letter for the city attorneys, letting them know about some incidents that he had to deal with concerning Jack. "Five incidents have been brought to my attention involving local women, three of which were contacts made as a result of police involvement," the chief wrote. They included a woman Jack had arrested for drunken driving; she later moved into his apartment. Another woman called police about someone slipping obscene photographs through a window. Jack had been the responding officer, and before long, they had struck up a relationship.

The chief said he personally had seen Jack's car parked all night outside her apartment.

Jack got involved with a third woman who worked for the city and was going through a divorce. The drama spilled over into loud barroom arguments with the woman's ex, the chief had written. There also was the woman he brought to a town party—she had been arrested for prostitution.

Jack also took topless photos of a 17-year-old waitress "in a Playboy-type pose."

"Tessier is not very well liked by his coworkers and several complaints have been received about his conduct from other police departments," the chief wrote. He added that Jack's infractions weren't serious.

"But," the chief said, "he is consistent in screwing up." Jack was soon rehired by the Milton Police Department.

In 1982, 14-year-old runaway Michelle Weinman was taken in by Officer Jack Tessier, who allowed her to sleep on his couch. She had left her father's home in Tacoma, Washington, as she had been skipping out of class in school and knew that he would punish her. One of Weinman's girlfriends, who decided to run away with her, told her about a friend of hers they could stay with. It was Jack.

The two girls ended up sleeping on a hideaway bed in Jack's living room. Jack became close to the girls and would take them to the movies, out to dinners, and shopping. Jack also taught them both how to drive in his police car. Jack almost became a father figure, teaching the girls how to use make-up and dress properly. He also made sure that they attended their classes in school.

Over the matter of weeks the girls stayed in Jack's apartment, he would also kiss them both good night at bedtime. Weinman also claimed that Jack gave her girlfriend a real "boyfriend kiss" one night. Weinman also claims that he would give them body massages, including their bottoms.

She said that she was molested by him back then. "I was on the couch. He just started to touch me, and tried to kiss me, and he assaulted me. This man is not what he claims to be. He wears a mask and it's scary."

In another report to CNN, Weinman also claimed that one night when she was sleeping, he woke her by whispering into her ear. Then, before she knew what was going on, he was performing oral sex on her. She said she couldn't stop it and just laid on the couch and was frozen with fear. She couldn't scream because she was so scared and ashamed.

Weinman later told her girlfriend about the encounter, who must have told a school counselor, who then later pulled Weinman out of class to be questioned by the police.

Jack was charged with statutory rape, but eventually plead guilty to communication with a minor for immoral purposes, which is a misdemeanor.

Jack defends this action only by saying that he didn't rape her. "I never attempted to rape her and I never had sex with her." Jack said he took the deal as he couldn't afford a lawyer. He ended up being placed on probation for one year. Jack then resigned from the police department on March 10, 1982.

REVIEW OF VIDEO OF QUESTIONING OF JACK MCCULLOUGH

I was contacted by the author, Alan Warren, in request to review part of the transcript of the questioning of a Jack McCullough by police detectives for the purpose pf ascertaining if, in my opinion, there were any indicators of deception in any of the subject's replies to the questions by the detectives.

I read the partial transcripts and, in my opinion, there was some evidence that some of the replies to some of the questions may have been deceptive. This, of course, is in no way indicative of the subject's innocence or guilt regarding the offense in question by the questioning detectives. It merely shows that there may have been some deception in some of his answers for whatever reason(s). I explained to the author that not being able to hear the answers and see the individual as he answered the questions presented by the detectives made it difficult to determine if there was or was not deception present in some or all of his answers. Not all deceptive indicators are syntaxual but can be verbal and physical as well. The author provided me with the video of the questioning of Jack McCullough by the detectives.

I reviewed the questioning video. During the questioning I observed and heard what, in my opinion, indicated additional indicators of deception regarding the answers to some of the questions. I observed numerous singular indicators of deception as well as incidents of indicator clustering during parts of the questioning. Clustering is when a subject answers a question and presents more than one indicator of deception and these clusters can consist of a combination of any or all indicators related to syntax, vocal, and physical. One such cluster occurred when the subject was asked about going on a date and, during his answer, (1) Repositioned in the chair suddenly, (2) Crossed his arms in front of his chest, and (3) Attempted to change the subject by inquiring how the information as read by the detective made him a suspect. A second cluster occurred when the subject was asked about alleged "sex play" with his sister. During that answer he (1) Invoked God, (2) Stammered, (3) Patted head and fidgeted with his hands on his head, (4) Exhibited signs of anger, and (5) Used more formal English eliminating contractions.

In my opinion, there appeared to be deceptive answers given by the subject to some of then questions posed by the detectives. As previously stated regarding the transcript review, these indicators **do not** prove or disprove the involvement of the subject in the crime in question and, in fact, may have nothing to do with that crime whatsoever. It may simply mean that the subject was simply not comfortable answering that particular question and/or providing that particular information.

About Steven David Lampley

Steven David Lampley is a former twenty-one year career police officer and SVU detective. Some of the cases on which he worked have been seen on television networks as Investigation Discovery, TruTV, Discovery Channel, and FOX. Steven worked closely with the Federal Bureau of Investigation, the United States Postal Inspector's Service, Department of Justice's United States Attorney's Office, and Attorney General Troy King (Alabama 2006-2011).

Steven now speaks and trains corporations, colleges and universities, organizations, and groups across the country on the techniques and indicators of detecting lies. Steven recently spoke at CrimeCon 2018 to a sold out audience with standing room only with 850 seated and has been a guest on Crime Stories with Nancy Grace. He is also the author of four true crime books, hosts the nationwide radio show and podcast *Crime & Forensics*, and is a contributing writer for *Law Enforcement Today*.

CHAPTER 13 — WHAT A WICKED GAME TO PLAY

"The worst thing about being lied to is knowing you weren't worth the truth." – *Turcois Ominek*

JEANNE TESSIER REPORT OF THE NIGHT MARIA WENT MISSING

The tragedy you carry is chained around your neck, the fate that you've been given.

When I was 9, Maria was kidnapped. She lived a block and a half away from me. She was 7. We had played together only occasionally—there were other kids closer at hand—and only when those we played with most often were unavailable did we venture further afield.

Maria was shy, quiet, sweet, small, and beautiful—dark eyes and hair, and somehow remote and inaccessible. Her closest friend was Kathy, who was 8 or 9 and lived on her street. Kathy was large, ungainly, unattractive. I knew them little, but I knew them. The first we knew of Maria's disappearance was when someone knocked on our side door on the snowy night she was taken. I was upstairs, but not asleep, and came down when I heard the knock. I heard men's voices talking to my father, asking him to open the hardware store where he worked so they could get flashlights and lanterns to look for her. My parents were keyed up. Mom told my sister and me that Maria had been kidnapped and that Dad was going to help look for her in the cornfields surrounding our town.

Meanwhile, women were gathering at the local armory to make sandwiches and coffee for the searchers.

It was about 9 o'clock at night. Dad jammed a 2-by-4 between the side door and the kitchen wall to keep it from being opened—there was no lock—and we were instructed to lock the front door behind them as they left and to sleep on the couch in the living room to let them in again when they came home, because they couldn't find the key. Dad helped the men. Mom joined the women.

I was awake for a long time after they left, my mind and body alive with that strange combination of adrenaline and terror that overtakes us when disasters strike. Finally, I slept, until the knock on the door that caused me to jump up in fear and peek through the door's small window, to see my mother's face there. I let her in. Dad was out all night, as were most of the men in town. Maria was not found.

No one spoke to us directly about what was going on, so my memories are of things I heard or overheard in conversations that did not include me. People spoke of nothing else. How much of what I heard was rumor and how much was true I do not know.

The search went on for days. The FBI came to town. An artist's rendering of Maria, in color, in a brown coat with a furry collar, missing one shoe, appeared in a Chicago newspaper. One of her shoes had been found near where she had last been seen, standing under a streetlight with her friend Kathy, just after dark. We heard that Kathy told police a man named Johnny had invited them to go for a ride and Kathy had said she'd have to go ask her mom. She left, and then Maria was gone. By the time they knew she was gone, the thick flakes of falling snow had nearly covered the footprints in the snow. I don't know if Kathy went back to the street corner, or how long it was before she told someone, or until Maria's parents looked for her and couldn't find her.

One evening a few days after Maria was gone, some FBI men came knocking at our door. My half-brother was 18. The men searched our home, upstairs, where my half-brother had slept in the anteroom at the top of the stairs and went through everything in his closet. Mom said they were looking for a bright-colored sweater that Maria's friend Kathy had described. They didn't find it. I thought I could tell from her profound agitation that my mother, too, wondered if "Johnny" was her own precious son.

Before the men left, they asked Mom what time our Johnny had gotten home the night Maria disappeared. She gave them a time. But he had not come home, not until sometime the next day. I knew by her lie that she suspected him, too. She told them he had been in a city nearby that day, enlisting in the armed services and that the recruiting officer with whom he had enlisted would vouch for him.

JEANNE HISTORY

According to Jeanne's memories from her self-written book, "Unspoken Truth" when she was a freshman in college, Jeanne was at a lecture where the professor started to explain about taboos in society. That day, her deep, dark secrets began to make sense. From an early age, she was traumatized and sexually abused by two members of her family. She was led to a therapist in her 20s by God. It seems that in Jeanne's mind, outside influences created these events right from the start.

As she tells us in her memoirs:

"I wonder if I was born with foreknowledge of the life I'd chosen, if I arrived, if perhaps we all arrive, with a prescient awareness that is present at birth but soon forgotten. One of the stories my mother used to tell was that I almost died when I was two months old. 'Double pneumonia,' she called it. Only the new wonder drug penicillin saved me. I was in the hospital for several weeks. It was Christmastime. I wonder if, seeing what was ahead, my spirit turned and ran, sure that I lacked the strength or will to survive the journey ahead. Maybe such fear and uncertainty are why we forget how it is we came to birth, and why. Or, as my original therapist believed, maybe my lungs were filled with my unshed tears.

"Another story Mom told, when I asked, was of my birth. The year she carried me, as she said, was the most miserable year of her life, with a hot and miserable summer that lasted well into fall. Did it occur to her that I might wonder if I was the reason for her misery? But I didn't wonder, because I was sure I was.

"She was reading a novel when she went into labor on that cool night in mid-October. She carried it with her to the hospital. She was so engrossed in the book that she was reluctant to be wheeled into the delivery room without it when I was ready to be born. At 4 am, as soon as I was born, she asked to be wheeled back to her room so she could finish her book.

"She went on to tell me that when she got back to her room, the sun was rising on a perfect autumn day—brilliant red and orange and yellow leaves ablaze on the trees outside her window and crystal blue sky overhead. 'What a beautiful day,' she said. 'And then I finished my book and went to sleep.' The morning of my birth was the first of many times, it seems, that me mother forgot about me. Twenty-five years or so from the day I was born, I sat in a therapy session with Taylor, a man whose name was given to me the year before by a friend named Pat on a day I'd said aloud that I needed one good reason not to kill myself. For four years, I saw Taylor.

"Once when I was nine or ten years old, I was in our living room and my father was dancing with and fingering my baby sister, who was less than one. On his face, a deranged and terrifying leer. He was laughing, smiling, and singing.

My baby sister was laughing, too, but anxiously. Her eyes connected with mine and I saw the panic and terror there. I wanted to stop him. I wanted to say something that would make him quit, but I was as afraid and powerless as I had been as a little child.

"When she knew she was dying but was still aware, my mother, one day out of nowhere, said to me, 'Do you know why I didn't do anything about what your father and brother did to you?' I said, 'No, but I'd sure like to know.' She said 'Because it's what my father and brothers did to me, and I thought it was just the way of the world.' She was right. It is. (But as Taylor would say, 'That's an explanation, but it's not an excuse.') What a moment of truth that was for me when Mom said those words. Finally, more than 40 years after my abuse began, clearing her slate as she prepared to die, Mom admitted that my story was true, and that it was her story, too. I felt both grateful and saddened to know that she'd known and looked away and that she, too, had suffered as a child. And what sad irony, that she'd run from her abusers and married one; a common tale. So, because the journey to the bathroom at night was full of danger, I'd awake with the need and then go back to sleep. And eventually I'd dream of getting up, of creeping down the stairs, of sitting on the toilet. Then I would awaken to wetness, at first thinking that I had forgotten to raise the toilet seat. As I came to the surface of consciousness, I'd realize with horror that I'd wet my bed.

"My parents got so angry when I wet my bed that when I did, I'd take off my clothes in the dark, find a dry spot on the bed, and curl up to sleep again. In the morning, I'd cover my bed with the blanket to hide my sin and sleep on that same polluted bedding again, though it was smelly and stiff, until I could sneak it down to the basement to be washed. I'm not sure when I stopped bed-wetting, but it may have been when the monster at the top of the stairs was thrown out of the house when he turned 16. I was eight. I was four when my half-brother brought his friend Dave over and ordered me to pull down my pants and lay on my bed so he could show his friend my genitals. I was mortified, and afraid of what would happen next, but Mom came home just then—I heard the back door slam as she came in—and I jumped up and ran downstairs and told her what had happened. She grimly ordered me to go into her bedroom and to stay there until she said I could come out. Then she called the boys downstairs, spoke to them in a whisper, and sent them outside.

"I waited and waited in her room for her to come for me, but she didn't. My brother was outside with his friend and I was in my parents' bedroom, isolated, waiting to be summoned. It was clear to me even at that time that I was the one being punished, and of course, in my shame,

I had already found myself to blame. This was the first of several times my brother shared me with a friend. When Dad came home for supper, I came out of the room. Mom said she had forgotten me.

"My Dad's abuses began in my infancy. They were abuses of preparation: fingering, stimulating, grinning, leering, and hungering for young flesh. My brother's began when I was four. When I was six years old, we moved for a year into a tiny country town with nothing more than a post office, a general store, a tavern, and 20 or so houses clustered nearby. My father was hired to manage the general store and we moved into an apartment above the store. My sister was eight, my half-brother 14, and my little brother was three.

"The apartment was small, and Mom was more miserable there than in our home, which was rented out while we were gone. It was there that my father fully raped me for the first time. 'I know what you want,' he angrily declared. 'I know what you're looking for.' He grabbed me by the arm and hauled me into a cornfield behind the tavern next door, threw me down on the dirt, and climbed aboard. When he left me there, I was covered in blood, my blue dress forever ruined, my heart broken, my soul ripped loose from its mooring. He went back to the store and I made my way back to the stairs that had been my ruin and the apartment above.

"My mother saw my bloody dress and demanded to know what I'd done. I told her what had been done to me. And she lost her mind, screaming at me, hitting me, calling me 'Liar! Liar!' She tore the dress over my head and arms and left me, naked and bereft, in my room. The dress was forever gone. And I was alone, sleep my escape, blood on my sheets, violated and blamed for my violation, denied my truth, all hope gone. My half-brother, Johnny, had sex with me for years. I was not his first and I was far from his last, but I was his for a very long time, when it suited him, when his hunger found no other outlet than me, who was close at hand.

"He molested other girls in the neighborhood before he got to me. One that I know of was the daughter of one of my mother's friends. When the friend came to talk to Mom about it, Mom did as she had done to me—she denied it, she closed the door, and she did not speak to or acknowledge her friend again for over a year, until the friend came to her and asked if they could put it behind them and move on.

"My aunt Mary had a theory which she shared with me when I was in my early teens. She believed that when he was eight or nine years old, he changed from a wonderful, lovable little boy into a monster. It happened, she believed, the day he was hit by a car on his way back to school after coming home for lunch. He was struck as he ran across the main street of town. He received a concussion that day, and my aunt believed it was the concussion that caused the change.

"Perhaps it was, but I have wondered for years what happened that day that made him late getting back to school. Was that the day someone first violated him? Did he witness my sister being violated? My mother never spoke of that accident and was angry that my aunt spoke of it to me. Why? Did she know why he ran in front of the car? There's so much I don't know and maybe never will, but whenever it happened, whether that day or another, my half-brother was indeed, a monster by the time he got his hands on me.

"The injuries he inflicted run so much deeper than those of my father and are so much harder to speak of, because my half-brother screwed not just my body but my mind. I was a child so desperately in need of love, and Johnny used that need in me to satisfy his own. At times, he even suggested that we might run away together and live where no one would know we were kin.

"He was Jekyll and Hyde; all words of love and tenderness on approach, telling me he couldn't help himself, begging me please, please, please to let him do the deed, promising kindness, gentleness, sweetness, but when aroused, delivering mindless animal rage. This pattern, which was set so early and so clearly, made me a co-conspirator because I allowed myself to surrender to his words. As a result, I hated and blamed myself for our relationship for many years. Each time I gave myself to him or allowed him to take me, I was left feeling brokenhearted and utterly betrayed.

"Dad threw Johnny out of the house when he was 16. He'd already been thrown out of school for something he said to his art teacher—I never knew what. He took a room in a home on the other end of town and got a job in a factory, then was back home briefly before he joined the service. My parents fought over Johnny so many times. Dad hated him, and Mom defended him against all comers. When Dad threw him out, he forbade him ever to 'set foot under this roof' again. But it didn't last.

"Once at least, while he was in the boarding house, he called Mom. I don't know what they spoke of, but she sent me to him to 'do his ironing'—me, alone, in a bedroom with him. Very little ironing got done. Did she know what she was doing? I don't know. Within a short time, he was thrown out of the boarding house, quit or was fired from his job, and came back home. Shortly thereafter, Maria disappeared, and Johnny joined the service and left for Texas.

"Once, when away, he wrote me a love letter. When my mother read it, she declared it rubbish and threw it away. When he came home once, more than four years later, he brought me a book. He was 21 or 22—I was 14. The book was 'The Collector,' by John Fowles. It is a novel about a man who kidnaps and keeps a woman. When he gave that book to me, he pronounced it 'the best book ever written.' When I read it, I was terrified. I understood then that his hunger was not for love or sex; it was hungering to control. I gave the book to Mom and asked her to read it. She did; I never saw it again.

"Home from the service, Johnny drifted again—a factory job, a house he rented with some other guys. One summer day, he drove by the house in a big red convertible. I don't know where he got it. It wasn't his. I was out front, and he stopped to say hello. He was a handsome young man, and the car was handsome, and I was young teenager bored on a summer day. I asked for a ride. He resisted at first—I was not the game he was hunting for that day, but I begged him— please, just a short ride. He let me in, drove me straight to the home he shared and fucked me. His friends came home and threw open the door to the room just as he was done. Without hesitation, he offered me to them. Two of the three took him up on the offer, the first one rolling me over and entering from behind, the next going for sloppy seconds. The third sat in the room with me for a little while and then told me to put my clothes on. I don't remember how I got home.

"The story doesn't end there. This dark and damaged soul went on to do harm to so many others. I wonder if all of them, like me, were fooled at first by his smooth-talking promises of love.

"Abusers and rapists, my half-brother among them, cast very wide nets and harm many. I will never fully recover from the harm he did to me.

"During the first semester of my freshman year in college, I was gang-raped at a fraternity party. A girl on my floor asked me to go as a blind date with a friend of her boyfriend who was coming in from out of town. I didn't want to do it, but finally allowed her to persuade me. When I got to the party, I was offered a glass of punch and soon was unable to think clearly or walk without assistance. I found myself being led out of the party and into a large dark room filled with mattresses separated from each other by sheets hanging from the ceiling. There I lay for I don't know how long, coming to consciousness at moments to find yet another dark figure on top of me. When I finally awoke, the house was still. I stumbled into my clothes, down some stairs and out the door, and began the long walk home.

"A month or so later, in late November, a high school classmate of mine who was attending the same university came to see me. He said he needed to talk. We were not good friends but I had always tried to be kind to him during our high school years when he was not a popular boy and was the butt of many jokes. We found a quiet place in one of the lounges of the dorm and he confessed to me that, as part of his fraternity initiation, he had been made to join in the gang-rape of a girl. I angrily asked him why he was telling this to me. He answered that he had to tell someone and that he was seeking forgiveness. I assured him he would get no forgiveness from me. He asked me what he should do, and I told him he would have to figure that out for himself. At the time, it didn't occur to me that perhaps the one he had gang-raped was me. I'll never know for sure, because he went home on Christmas break a week and hung himself from a rafter in his family home. It is not only the victims who are victimized by cultures of abuse. When I learned of his death, I was so sorry I hadn't been kinder just one more time."

Jack McCullough at age 17

CHAPTER 14 — RAPE TRIAL OF JEANNE TESSIER

From the "48 Hours" TV program with Erin Moriarty:

"Did you abuse your sister when you were growing up?" Erin asked Jack. After a long pause, and while Jack stared into Erin's eyes Erin continued, "You did, didn't you?"

After the pause, Jack said, "Me and my sister were very close."

"What do you mean, you were very close with your sister?"

Jack interrupted with, "We're done with this. This has nothing to do with Maria. It has nothing to do with murder."

A short pause happened between the two and Erin began again with, "You—"

Jack sharply and firmly cut her off again with, "We're done!"

"So, you're not going to answer anything anymore?" Erin asked.

"Correct!"

Because the former district attorney, Clay Campbell, didn't feel comfortable enough to take Jack to trial for the kidnapping and murder of Maria Ridulph, he thought it would be better to charge and convict Jack of the rape of his very own sister. With that rape against Jack, he thought for sure that he would have enough to sway a jury that Jack had also kidnapped and murdered Maria.

It was 10 years later when his sister told the police both her father and Jack had abused her for years when she was young. Jeanne claimed that her sister, Katherine, would send her to their father to be raped several times. It was also during the interview with Jeanne that she told Brion Hanley, the detective on the case from the Illinois State Police, that their mother had lied to the FBI about Jack being home on the night Maria disappeared.

The former DA, Clay Campbell, said that he would never charge Jack or tell anybody about this. But within a short time, he came back to her and told her he was sorry—that even though he had already told her he would never charge Jack, he was going ahead with exactly that.

Jeanne Tessier (Jack's sister)

She then elaborated on one specific time, when Jack had returned on leave from military duty one summer. Jack drove up to their house in a big red convertible. Jeanne said that she didn't know where he got the car, but he was a very handsome young man, and the car was handsome as well. Jeanne then asked if he would give her a ride in the new car, and at first he was hesitant, but eventually agreed. Jeanne commented, "I was not the game he was hunting for that day, but I begged him, please, just a short ride. He let me in, drove me straight to the home he shared and fucked me. His friends came home and threw open the door to the room just as he was done. Without hesitation, he offered me to them. Two of the three took him up on the offer, the first one rolling me over and entering from behind, the next going for sloppy seconds. The third sat in the room with me for a little while and then told me to put my clothes on. I don't remember how I got home."

But in court, Jeanne was not a good witness to have on the stand. Jeanne could not remember if the rape happened in summer or what time of year it was, for that matter. The only thing that she could slightly remember was that she didn't have school that day. Was this a faulty memory or was it that she was blocking it all out as it was a traumatic experience?

The other issue in court was that nobody else could remember Jack ever having a convertible. This included not only Jack himself, but all of Jack's friends and family. Jeanne described the car as a red Mustang. Someone should have told the prosecution, before the defense told them, that Mustangs did not come out until 1964. It is hard to go for a ride in a car that does not exist.

One of the biggest inconsistencies was also why Jeanne would ever ask for a ride, let alone beg for a ride, from the brother who constantly sexually abused her throughout her youth? If he were one of the constant abusers in the house, along with their father, why would she be trying to spend any time with him at all?

Another issue Jeanne and the prosecutor had was her description of the house that Jack took her to and raped her. She kept changing how the house looked, with hallways that never existed, and even how she got home.

Per the court documents:

Mr. Clay Campbell: "Did you walk down a hallway?"

Jeanne Tessier: "Yes."

Actually, he asked her twice. Then, she spent most the trial describing the room in the front of the house. The prosecution was so entirely sloppy in their case they did not even check the layout of the house. The defense team went in the house, and really made a fool of everyone.

In trial, Jeanne was able to describe the neighborhood that the house was in and also talked about her walk home. *"I had not been in that neighborhood before and I wasn't sure I could find my way home, but I began walking and finally I saw the entrance to the Elmwood Cemetery, which is a place I had been before. And I then knew I could get home from there."*

Another issue for Clay Campbell was trying to find the other three guys that Jeanne claimed raped her that day in the house. They were not able to do that. The guys who lived in the house back in the time of the rape also testified that not only had Jack never lived with them, they never ever saw Jeanne before, and nobody had ever been raped in their house.

There is also another thought, in a small, close-knit community like Sycamore, the family's mother was a stay-at-home housewife whose duties included cooking the family dinner, where the whole family would all eat together. But if the rape happened the way that Jeanne described it, can you imagine a 14-year-old girl being raped several times by at least three men, and her walking home to have dinner with the family, and nobody noticed? Jeanne also said that there was nobody at home when she returned after the rape, that she took a shower and went from the basement to her room in a towel. Again, this was another unlikely scenario with five siblings all living at home and two parents, one of whom never worked outside of the home.

Judge Robbin Stuckert delivered a blistering rebuke to prosecutors for failing to ask basic questions of the accuser, a 64-year-old woman who came forward to testify against her half-brother, Jack McCullough, more than four decades later. Stuckert talked about fading memories and the doubt created by the woman's description of a car driven by McCullough that nobody else who testified recalled ever seeing.

"The state has failed to meet their burden," she said. A visibly angry DeKalb state's attorney Clay Campbell would not discuss what problems McCullough's acquittal might create when the 72-year-old stood trial for the 1957 kidnapping and slaying of Maria Ridulph, a case that stirred the nation half a century ago.

McCullough's public defender, Regina Harris, said the slaying case against her client might have been that much stronger had he been convicted of rape.

"It takes a factor away from them they would have had," she said.

McCullough's acquittal in the rape case after a two-day bench trial before the judge also raises questions about whether prosecutors would push to have another judge for the murder trial or whether Harris would again insist that a judge, and not a jury, decide her client's fate.

Both attorneys declined to discuss strategy for the next trial.

McCullough showed no emotion in court when the verdict was announced on that Thursday, but Harris said he cried afterward.

"He's relieved to tears," she said.

McCullough had been charged with rape and indecent liberties with a child in Sycamore in 1962. The accuser, McCullough's half-sister Jeanne Tessier, testified she was 14 when McCullough picked her up in a convertible and drove her to an unfamiliar house, where he assaulted her in a dark room before two other men also raped her.

The Associated Press generally does not name victims in rape cases, but Tessier gave reporters permission to use her name and talked openly about the alleged incident in an article published online in 2010.

Prosecutors argued McCullough took advantage of the teen while he held a position of authority and trust. Defense attorneys said no one could corroborate Jeanne's story and that there was no physical evidence.

Another woman (Michelle Weinman) testified that she was sexually assaulted by McCullough in 1982 when he was a police officer in Milton, Washington, and she was a 15-year-old runaway. McCullough originally was charged with statutory rape, eventually pleaded guilty to unlawful communication with a minor, and was fired from his job.

Stuckert criticized prosecutors for their failure to ask Jeanne during trial why she didn't come forward until a few years ago. The judge said they also failed to present evidence that might have supported her allegations, such as a change in her behavior, grades, or appearance that one might expect after such a traumatic experience.

"The state simply did not ask," she said.

Campbell was livid at the suggestion, saying the judge had prohibited him from presenting certain evidence, including allegations of other sexual incidents.

"The judge barred us from going into that information," he said.

Jeanne, now living in Kentucky, was not in court when the verdict was read, but other family members were. Even a half-hour after the verdict was announced, they remained visibly upset, squeezing each other's hands, with Jeanne's brother, Bob, hugging a sheriff's deputy on the way out the door, saying, "We'll get the bastard the next time."

Maria Ridulph's older brother, Chuck, also was emotional. "He will have to answer one day to God," he said.

McCullough was being held on the Ridulph charges on more than $3 million bond in the DeKalb County jail, about 65 miles West of Chicago.

Jeanne had come forward after McCullough was arrested in Maria's death, one of the oldest slaying cases in the nation to be reopened.

Maria was abducted as she played outside her home in December 1957. Her body was found the following spring in a wooded area about 120 miles away.

McCullough, who was 18 and went by the name John Tessier at the time, lived less than two blocks from her home. He was an initial suspect but had an alibi: he said he had traveled to Chicago that day for military medical exams before enlisting in the Air Force.

Maria's body was exhumed that same month to check for DNA evidence, but none could be found. However, a forensic anthropologist found that Maria had been stabbed in the throat at least three times by a long, sharp blade, pointing out the nicks in her sternum and neck vertebrae, consistent with at least three slashes to the throat. Although stabbing was considered the likely cause of death, an appellate court later stated that the findings did not preclude other possible causes of death such as ligature strangulation, which could not be determined due to the decomposition of soft tissue.

News of the arrest in a 54-year-old murder case drew national attention. The lead prosecutor, DeKalb County state's attorney Clay Campbell, was reluctant to take the case due to its age and the lack of any physical evidence connecting McCullough to the crime, but after being persuaded by the Ridulph and Tessier families, who all believed that McCullough was guilty, he formally charged Jack with the kidnapping and murder of Maria Ridulph.

The trial for the kidnapping and murder of Maria Ridulph began. Numerous witnesses testified for the prosecution, including Maria's family members, neighbors, law enforcement personnel, and Kathy Sigman (now Chapman), who was the star witness and identified McCullough as "Johnny," the man who had walked up to her and Maria 50 years earlier. Another friend of Maria's testified that she had also been offered a piggyback ride from "Johnny" and identified him as McCullough.

Three inmates who were jailed with McCullough testified that Jack had talked about killing Maria to them. However, their stories were inconsistent and failed to match the evidence indicating that Maria had been stabbed. One inmate said McCullough told him that he had strangled Maria with a wire, and another inmate said that McCullough accidentally smothered Maria to stop her from screaming.

The defense argued that the prosecutors and police were pressured by the Ridulph and Tessier families to solve the case and implicate McCullough, although there was no physical evidence, motive, or indication that Jack was even in the area when Maria was kidnapped. McCullough did not take the stand in his own defense on the advice of his attorneys.

On September 14, 2012, Jack McCullough was convicted of the kidnapping and murder of Maria Ridulph. He received a life sentence with the possibility of parole after 20 years. He was 73 years old at the time of sentencing.

CHAPTER 15 — RICHARD SCHMACK, I NEED A HERO

Richard Schmack the Dekalb County State's Attorney who drove the release of Jack McCullough

Richard Schmack was the DeKalb County State's Attorney was honored by the American Bar Association for his work on Jack McCullough's post-conviction case. The now former state's attorney had independently investigated Jack's conviction from the December 3, 1957, murder case of Maria Ridulph, which led to the release and granting of a certificate of innocence by Judge William Brady on April 12, 2016.

Schmack used FBI reports from the 1950s compiled after Maria's disappearance in Sycamore and evidence that McCullough used a pay phone in Rockford about the time she last was seen. Schmack, who is semi-retired, working in private practice and lives in Sycamore, will receive the Norm Maleng Minister of Justice Award from the American Bar Association Justice Section at its fall meeting Nov. 3, 2018, in Washington, D.C. The award is named after Maleng, a former King County, Washington, prosecutor who embodied the tenets of the ABA standards for criminal justice, according to the release. McCullough lives in Seattle, which happens to be in King County.

Jack McCullough, convicted in the oldest cold case ever brought to court, broke into a wide grin as a judge ordered him released from prison on April 12, 2016, and granted him a new trial. Jack McCullough, at this time 76, was serving a life sentence for the 1957 murder of 7-year-old Maria Ridulph. Judge William Brady threw out the conviction after a prosecutor found "clear and convincing evidence" that McCullough was wrongly found guilty.

He was freed shortly after the hearing and was whisked away in a car driven by a family member. After the judge's ruling, McCullough turned toward his stepdaughter, Janey O'Connor, and flashed her a private signal that she says meant "I love you." She was seated behind him and broke into tears but managed a big smile back. Across the aisle, Charles Ridulph, the older brother of the victim, frowned and bowed his head. More than 58 years ago, he helped search for Maria after she vanished from a street corner near their home while playing in the snow with a friend. McCullough's lawyers and DeKalb

County state's attorney Richard Schmack argued that McCullough's conviction was based on false testimony, improper legal rulings controlling the evidence presented, and a timeline that was tweaked some 50 years after the fact to rule out McCullough's alibi.

McCullough has long insisted that he couldn't possibly have abducted and killed the child because he was 40 miles away in Rockford, Illinois, talking to recruiters and trying to enlist in the U.S. Air Force, when she was taken. He repeated the alibi when he spoke with CNN from prison in March 2013. "They proved nothing," he said at the time. "I am in here for murder. A murder I would not, could not have done." McCullough said that when Maria was kidnapped, the telephone in his home in Sycamore was ringing. "And I was on the other end of that phone, in Rockford, three minutes before she was kidnapped. Try and make that happen. Only Scotty could make that happen, if he beamed me up."

An Illinois appeals court upheld his conviction 2016 But McCullough made a last-ditch appeal in a jailhouse motion last December, saying police and prosecutors buried evidence supporting his alibi. He asked a judge to find him innocent. Schmack, who inherited the case from predecessor Clay Campbell, was placed in the position of having to defend the conviction.

He launched a six-month investigation that included a review of some 4,500 pages of documents—old police and FBI reports, grand jury transcripts, trial transcripts, affidavits for search and arrest warrants, and even CNN's five-part series on the case, "Taken," which raised questions about whether the courtroom reconstruction of history was unfairly one-sided. Schmack concluded that he'd found "clear and convincing evidence" that McCullough had been convicted of a crime he didn't commit. The precise time of Maria's abduction has been in dispute almost from the beginning.

The first thing Jack McCullough did as a free man was order a slice of pizza. For years, he'd practically drool every time a pizza commercial came on the tiny television in his cell at Illinois' Pontiac Correctional Center, where he was serving the life term he was sentenced to for a murder he's always insisted he didn't commit.

Finally, on Friday, April 15, 2017, a judge agreed that his murder trial had been so flawed that McCullough should go free. It took a minute for the news to register. When it did, McCullough sighed with relief and then grinned from ear to ear. He turned toward the muscular, shiny-pated man guarding him and raised his wrists, ready for unshackling. But he'd have to wait a little longer to be processed out of the system.

Two hours later, his stepdaughter, Janey O'Connor, was gunning a white rental car out of the parking lot of the jail across the street from the DeKalb County Courthouse. In the back seat was McCullough and Crystal Harrolle, the investigator from the public defender's office. Harrolle had also been by

McCullough's side in court in September 2012, when people had stood and cheered the guilty verdict in what was touted as the oldest cold case to go to trial. Tears flooded his eyes as he recalled being told afterward how Harrolle walked out of court and sat in her car and cried.

But she never gave up on him, and neither did O'Connor. And so, heads spinning, they drove around the corner to World Famous Pizza, and McCullough bit into a slice of pepperoni. After years of prison food, including a meal he called "kinda pizza," it was the best thing he'd ever tasted.

"A guy came out of the Harley shop next door and he cranked it. And I said, 'Free-dom!'" McCullough paused and laughed, savoring the memory. "It was a wonderful feeling."

Maria Ridulph's murder went unsolved for half a century. Then, detectives pursued a tip and a man was brought to trial and convicted in the 1957 murder of the 7-year-old in Sycamore, Illinois. Now, that man is free.

McCullough was still riding the high a couple of hours later when he granted CNN his first exclusive interview as a free man. He had spoken with the network once before, from prison shortly after his conviction, for the CNN digital series "Taken," which examined his murder trial and raised questions about whether it was fair.

This time, he was elated and a bit overwhelmed, but didn't seem angry or bitter. Perhaps that would come later. But not now. "I'm just perceiving everything. I'm seeing, I'm feeling, I'm talking," he said. "I am glad to be out. I feel compassion for the people who are still there. I just want them to know I didn't escape from anything. I wasn't guilty in the first place."

And so, he persisted. "I just never gave up. I knew I was innocent," he said. "I knew I had proof that I was innocent, and I was going to make them see the proof, one way or the other." He seems in remarkably good shape for a 76-year-old, much less one who has been locked up since June 29, 2011—the day he was arrested in Seattle. "I didn't think this day would come," he added. "I was beginning to believe I couldn't get justice in Illinois. But here it is." Justice is still unfolding for McCullough. Although he is free, he technically could stand trial once again. State's attorney Richard Schmack, who is convinced McCullough is innocent, says he isn't finished with this case. Schmack motioned in April 2016, to dismiss the murder charge with prejudice, meaning nobody can ever again bring McCullough into court and accuse him of murdering his 7-year-old neighbor, Maria Ridulph.

And so, everybody prepared for court, again on a Friday. After that, McCullough may finally be free to return home to Seattle, where his wife, Sue, has been waiting for him. "I've got another week to go to sort out whatever legal matters are pending, and then I can go home to my wife and start my life over and do as much good in life as I've got left," he said. "The next 10 years of my life are gonna be at 100 miles an hour because I've got a hell of a lot to do."

When CNN spoke with McCullough from prison in March 2013, he was moved to tears just once, when he recalled his combat experience in Vietnam. Now, he gets misty-eyed often, usually while talking about the people who have helped him or stood by him. He is embarrassed by his tears, but powerless to stop them as he processes his newfound freedom.

Jack McCullough's freedom didn't come as the result of legal razzle-dazzle, although at the end he was represented by a trio of lawyers from a top Chicago law firm. McCullough calls them his "rock-star lawyers." But they were brought in late in the game to spiff up his own jailhouse lawyering. He had exhausted all his appeals and didn't have a lawyer when he filed a handwritten petition prepared by another inmate with paralegal training.

That was in June, and a judge in Sycamore tossed his petition out of court, calling it "frivolous" and "without merit." But it caught the attention of Harrolle and her boss, DeKalb Public Defender Tom McCulloch, who had represented McCullough at trial and believed he had been wrongfully convicted. Schmack, who knew he could eventually be tasked with defending the conviction, decided he'd better dig into the 4,500-page discovery file. It included old FBI, Illinois State Police, and local sheriff's investigative reports from 1957 and 1958.

Schmack took them home and started looking through them in his spare time.

He'd attended the trial in 2012; he was in private practice and running against state's attorney, Clay Campbell, who was personally prosecuting the case in court. Schmack told CNN he was troubled by how thin the evidence was.

McCullough, meanwhile, was undaunted. He filed a second handwritten petition on December 11. This time, his former public defender joined in, saying that while the crafting of the do-it-yourself petition was "inartful," some of the issues raised had "constitutional merit." He asked the court to appoint a lawyer to help McCullough with his appeal. He even volunteered to do it himself.

The judge asked Schmack for a response to the petition. Schmack stunned everyone by filing a lengthy, heavily footnoted report that he said demonstrated "clear and convincing evidence" McCullough was innocent.

He attached exhibits supporting his footnotes—grand jury transcripts and some of the FBI reports that had been barred from McCullough's trial.

As the appeal moved forward at the courthouse in Sycamore, it presented an ironic reverse scenario: An inmate's handwritten petition had resulted in a prosecutor admitting to nearly three dozen facts and allegations raised by the defendant. "I was ordered to file an answer, and I could not file an answer that denied his claim of actual innocence when I actually believe he is not guilty of the crime he was convicted of," Schmack explained. "The only question was whether I filed something very brief and cryptic or something more extensive. So, my feeling was the public has the right to know why

I was doing what I was doing, and why I was not answering this in the conventional way."

Chicago attorneys Gabe Fuentes and Shaun Van Horn, who work for a large, prestigious firm that seeks exoneration for wrongfully convicted defendants, agreed to represent McCullough through the rest of his appeal.

In court on that Friday, Fuentes, a former federal prosecutor, told Judge William Brady in no uncertain terms: "This was a prosecution that went off the rails. There are deep, deep problems with this case, which is why Mr. Schmack has come before this court with his report on those errors."

He went further, stating that the trial court and the appeals court were misled about the evidence against McCullough. At the trial, only a vague time frame was offered for when the little girl was abducted from a Sycamore street corner near her home. And, he said, evidence clearly establishing McCullough's whereabouts that evening was kept out of the trial. That evidence supported the alibi McCullough had claimed all along.

Schmack cited an ethical code that became law in January 2017. It lays on prosecutors a duty to undo wrongful convictions when they find them. "Most people who are innocent and get exonerated in this country don't get exonerated on appeal," Schmack said in court. "They get exonerated at proceedings like this. If the standard was that we can't look beyond the rulings that were made on appeal, they'd never be exonerated."

Brady, the judge, relied on three key items of evidence in throwing out McCullough's conviction. Two were discovered after the trial, and the other had been barred by a faulty evidentiary ruling at the trial.

Freshly subpoenaed phone records placed the pay phone used for the 6:57 p.m. collect call to McCullough's parents at the post office in Rockford—just where he said he was at the time the girl was snatched on December 3, 1957. The records supported McCullough's alibi, which he was unable to present at his murder trial.

If McCullough were indeed 40 miles away from the crime scene, Brady said, doubt would be cast on the testimony of Kathy Chapman, Maria's playmate. She picked McCullough out of a photo lineup some 50 years after the fact, saying he was the man who called himself "Johnny" and offered the girls piggyback rides minutes before Maria was last seen. Brady also found that the trial and appeals courts did not yet know about an inmate's allegations that prosecutors offered him favorable treatment with his own case if he testified against McCullough. "Those are matters that go to the heart of this prosecution," Brady said. "Each, by itself, may not have affected the outcome of the trial," he added, "but when viewed collectively, they make it unlikely that McCullough would have been convicted." There was no one in court to speak for the people who investigated and prosecuted the case against McCullough. Campbell, the former state's attorney, and the Illinois State Police had declined repeated requests for comment. The judge took pains to say on the record that he personally knew both Campbell and Schmack and didn't view the controversy over the case as politically motivated.

McCullough said his nearly five years behind bars had led him to believe that at least 5 percent of his fellow inmates are also not guilty. But many of his fellow prisoners considered him guilty—and for the worst of crimes. Making things even more dangerous for him in prison was his own law enforcement background. "I'm a former policeman and a convicted child killer, and by extension they would think child molester, whatever," he said. "In prison, that's a death sentence." A man must take precautions to stay safe. McCullough kept a low profile and worked at not offending anyone. "I have spent all of my time in prison in protective custody with guards protecting me from the inmates. I refrained from going outside a lot, because outside is where you are with everybody and anybody can hand you something steely and unpleasant. So, I stayed in my cell a lot. Not because I was afraid, but because it was the smartest thing to do." He was attacked by a cellmate during his first year in prison. The man stabbed him in the eye with the sharpened handle of a toothbrush. The next day, every toothbrush in the prison was confiscated.

He said he believes he was deliberately placed with a man who guards knew would attack him. But the inmate was a "small" guy and "he wasn't a threat to me if I was awake," McCullough said. "But I'm asleep and he has a sharp object and he's stabbing me in the face and head and eye. I took two stitches to the back of my eye. I was a bloody mess, and the blood behind my eye pushed my eye out. I pushed my eye back in and blood squirted across the room. And I was just covered in blood. And what for?" he asked. "He wanted to blind me. He knew I loved to read." He praised the medical care he received, saying he eventually recovered his vision. He showed off a semicircular scar on the meaty part of his hand. "Those are teeth marks," he said. "When I snatched the toothbrush out of his hand, he grabbed my hand and bit me." McCullough tried to throw the toothbrush out of the cell, but it kept bouncing off the door. "So, I kept kicking him until the guards came. Nobody was going to say a word. They usually just let fights go. But as soon as I said, 'He's stabbing me,' everybody showed up." Quarters can be overwhelming, McCullough says.

He did what he could to preserve his own humanity. He snipped the wires off a pair of ear buds and used them to dull the sounds of men screaming. It didn't completely silence them, but at least he could no longer make out what they were saying.

And he sought solace in the prison library, where he says he could at least find some "intelligent people." He studied languages, including Mandarin and Japanese. "When I first arrived in prison, everybody said, 'Go hit the law books.' Well, I'm not a lawyer. I don't want to be a lawyer, and I'm not going to get myself out of prison," he said. Instead, he befriended an inmate who had trained as a paralegal. McCullough teared up as he described how the man helped him frame his appeals, even writing them out by hand in tidy block letters because there were no typewriters in the prison. "He helped me, and he started to file motions for me, and the next thing I knew I was getting results," McCullough said. "And I'm tickled pink." His attorneys have advised him not to talk to the media or discuss anything related to his court cases. But he places prosecutor Schmack in a different category. He was among the people who assisted him, even though the prosecutor technically holds the power to put him back behind bars.

CHAPTER 16 — FBI TIMELINE REPORT

"Lying is a cooperative act. Think about it. A lie has no power whatsoever by its mere utterance. Its power emerges when someone else agrees to believe the lie." – Pamela Meyer

One of the biggest issues with the trial was the fact that the judge never allowed the FBI files as evidence in the case. This was done after he ruled that it was hearsay.

December 3, 1957, Sycamore, IL.

3:30 to 3:35 p.m.: Maria and Kathy leave West School and go across the street to Kathy's house at 644½ Archie Place. There, they played while waiting for Kathy's blue jeans to dry in Mrs. Sigman's electric dryer (SAO-2685, SAO-2581).

4 p.m. (about): Kathy and Maria leave for Maria's house. Along the way, they stop at Cecelia Davy's house at 644 Archie Place, directly in front of the Sigman home, where they pick up empty orange juice cans to use in making Christmas decorations for school (SAO-2685).

4 p.m. (shortly after): Maria and Kathy arrive at the Ridulph house (SAO-2685).

4 to 5 p.m. (about): The girls play at the Ridulph house, cutting out paper snowflakes and working on decorations for Christmas. Sometime during the hour, the girls go to Ferguson's West End Grocery to buy candy. Also during the hour, the girls made plans to play outside in the season's first snowfall after supper. They asked Mrs. Ridulph for permission (SAO-2708), which apparently wasn't granted at that time (SAO-2779, SAO-2586). It is likely, since the girls made plans to go outside after supper, that the snow had started falling sometime before 5 p.m.

5 p.m. (about): The Ridulphs began eating supper (SAO-2708, implied).

5 to 5:30 p.m. (about): Kathy went home for supper (SAO-2685). Paperboy Joseph Jones saw her leave the Ridulphs' headed toward her home (SAO-2906).

5:30 p.m. (about): The Sigmans began eating supper (trial transcripts, page 148).

5:30 p.m.: Ridulph family finished supper (SAO-2703). Sometime after supper, Maria was given permission to play outside with Kathy. She rushed to the telephone, called Kathy, and excitedly exclaimed, "I can go outside tonight! Can you?" Maria told her mother she and Kathy were going to play "up at the corner—at the big tree." (SAO-2708)

5:41 p.m. (about): Randy Strombom finished his paper route. As he rode his bike past the corner on his way home at 610 Archie Place, he saw no one (SAO-2906).

5:45 p.m. (about): Mr. Thomas Cliffe, 503 Center Cross, called Tom Braddy's wife, who in turn called her husband as he was preparing to leave work at the Standard Oil yard on North Main Street. Mr. Cliffe had requested a delivery of heating oil. Mr. Braddy left immediately after receiving the call for the Cliffes' house at 503 Center Cross (SAO-2787).

5:50 p.m. (about): Tom Braddy arrived in front of the Cliffe house, parking his truck on the West side of Center Cross, facing South, with the truck's back end protruding slightly into the intersection at Archie Place. He turned on his parking lights and his floodlights, aiming them toward the back of the Cliffes' house at the oil service point. He began unwinding hoses and setting up for delivery of the heating oil. He delivered 200 gallons from three tanks, requiring that he change hoses twice during the delivery. The delivery rate was 20 gallons/minute, and with setup time plus time to change hoses twice, plus the time to stow everything away after completing his service call, it can be estimated that Braddy was at the corner for about 20 minutes. He looked at his watch before driving away. It read 6:15 p.m. (SAO-2787).

5:50 p.m.: Maria Ridulph went outside (time established by Frances Ridulph, Maria's mother). She walked west along Archie toward Kathy's house. It was snowing, so she likely played in the snow a house or two east of Kathy's as she waited for Kathy to come outside (SAO-2703). The phone call from Maria was cited by Kathy on SAO-2979 to have occurred at 6:01 p.m.

6:02 p.m. (about): Kathy left her home after being given permission to go outside and play with Maria. She met Maria a house or two east of her own. From there, the girls walked east toward the street corner (SAO-2999).

6 to 6:05 p.m.: Frances Ridulph left the house with her daughter, Kay. Both saw Maria and Kathy Sigman together in the front yard starting to walk to the corner of Archie Place and Center Cross Street. Both Kay and her mother saw Mr. Braddy's truck parked on Center Cross (SAO-2703, 2719).

6 to 6:15 p.m.: H.E. "Tom" Braddy delivered oil to the Cliffe home on the corner of Archie Place and Center Cross Street. During the delivery, the girls arrived and began playing, skipping and jumping over his hoses, and talking with Mr. Braddy as he walked back and forth through the Cliffes' yard during the oil delivery. He checked his watch as he left the corner. It read 6:15 p.m. The girls were playing alone on the corner at this time (SAO-741, 2786, 2787).

6 to 6:30 p.m. (about): Mrs. Aldena Cliffe of 503 Center Cross, the corner where the girls were playing, said she heard girls playing outside her house (SAO-2782). Mr. Thomas Cliffe said he heard the girls playing outside sometime between 6 and 7 p.m. (SAO-2785).

6:05 p.m. (about): David Strombom, 610 Archie Place, arrived home from his work as sales manager at Fargo Motors (437 (?) West State Street) for supper. He saw Tom Braddy's truck parked at the corner but did not see the girls (SAO-2777).

6:05 to 6:20 p.m. (about): The Stromboms—David, wife Meredith, and son Randy—ate supper (SAO-2793).

6:15 p.m. (about): Frances Ridulph returned home and saw Maria and Kathy playing on the corner. They were alone. She waved at Maria, who waved back. Mrs. Ridulph cannot recall if Mr. Braddy's truck was still parked at the corner (SAO-2703).

6:15 p.m. (about): Sycamore High School basketball coach Neil Hudson dismissed practice early because he wanted to go to DeKalb to watch the local high school team play a scheduled game that night. Sycamore had an upcoming game against DeKalb the following Saturday, December 7. Coach Hudson said that everyone had left the high school between 6:30 to 6:45 p.m. (SAO-2754).

6:15 to 7:15 p.m. (about): Kay had her voice lesson at instructor Madge Wright's, 216½ W. State Street (SAO-2739).

6:20 p.m. (about): Braddy passed Tige Hoffman's Texaco at 531 DeKalb Avenue (now the location of Fire Station #1) on his way back to the Standard Oil yard on North Main. He noticed the time on the clock outside the station reading 6:20 p.m. (SAO-741).

6:25 p.m. (about): Neighbor Randy Strombom, having just finished his supper, went next door to listen to records with Chuck Ridulph in their den (SAO-2793).

6:30 p.m. (slightly before): Basketball team members Ed Boies (303 Center Cross, SW corner of Roosevelt Court and Center Cross) and another player with the last name Albright left the high school in a car driven by Kent Bellendorf of 741½ DeKalb Avenue (NE corner of DeKalb and Center Cross) on their way home after basketball practice (SAO-2751, 2754).

6:30 p.m. (exactly): Mr. Ridulph, who had been reading the newspaper, turned on television and began watching "Cheyenne," an hour-long western, on ABC. It is likely, because of better reception, that he was watching WREX Channel 13 out of Rockford and not WBKB Channel 7 out of Chicago. Mrs. Ridulph sat down with the newspaper in the first-floor bedroom. Daughter Pat was doing homework at the kitchen table. Chuck and Randy were listening to records in the den near the side door (SAO-2704, 2710).

6:30 p.m. (exactly): David and Meredith Strombom began watching "Name That Tune," a half-hour game show, on CBS, WBBM Channel 2, out of Chicago (SAO-2793).

6:30 p.m. (exactly): Mr. Elmer Westburg, 412 Center Cross Street, began watching "Cheyenne" with his two grandchildren (SAO-2781).

6:30 p.m.: Clayton West, driver for the DeKalb-Sycamore Bus Line, passed the corner headed south. Archie Place and Center Cross was a stop along his route. There were no passengers signaling to get off and he saw no one at the corner waiting to board, so he passed by without stopping. Mr. West didn't see the girls or anyone else at the corner (SAO-2938).

6:30 p.m. (about): Ken Davy, accompanied by Mr. and Mrs. Bobby Roy Peifer, saw the girls playing alone on the corner as they drove east along Archie Place to the stop sign at the corner. They not only saw the girls, but they engaged one another in conversation about whether the girls should be outside playing alone on the corner after dark. Ken Davy knew both girls. The Peifers did not. Ken Davy was helping the Peifers move into the upstairs apartment of his parents' home at 644 Archie Place (SAO-2669, 2674, 2777, 2778).

6:30 p.m. (or slightly after): Kent Bellendorf arrived home with passenger Ed Boies after dropping off another passenger, Albright (full name unknown), at his home. Bellendorf parked in the garage behind his home and went immediately inside. Boies left the garage immediately and headed for his home at 303 Center Cross. He walked north up the east side of Center Cross, then crossed diagonally to the west side in the vicinity of Archie Place, then on to his home another block north. Ed Boies saw no one, nor did he see any automobiles on his walk home from the Bellendorf residence. As Boies entered the front door of his home, he looked at the clock on the wall opposite the door. Both hands were pointing straight down, indicating 6:30 p.m. or possibly a minute or two after (SAO-2751, 2753, 2754). (Note: Ed Boies is the cousin of the famous attorney David Boies, who represented Al Gore in Bush v. Gore. He also argued the marriage equality case before the Supreme Court. David Boies was born in Sycamore and lived there until sometime in his grammar school years. The family then moved to California.)

6:30 p.m. (or slightly after): Larry Wilkins, 628 Roosevelt Court, along with dinner guests Jerry, Roger, and David Taylor went outside to play in the Wilkins' back yard. From their back yard, they had a clear view of the sidewalk on Archie Place under the streetlight in front of the residence at 631 Archie (SAO-2783, 2816).

6:30 to 6:35 p.m.: An unknown individual approached the two girls on the corner, greeted them, told them his name was "Johnny," and asked if they liked dolls and piggyback rides. He offered both girls a piggyback ride; only Maria accepted. He gave Maria a short ride and brought her back to the corner. Johnny asked Maria if she had a doll she could show him. Maria ran home to get one. Kathy estimated in 1957 that Johnny arrived 15 minutes after Tom Braddy left the corner (SAO-2691, 2979, 3000).

6:30 to 7 p.m.: Sometime during this half-hour, Mrs. Stanley (Barbara) Wells looked out of her window and saw two children with an unknown individual she believed to be an adult. They were playing around the big tree on the corner in the Cliffes' front yard. She said the adult was about 5'5" to 5'6", based on the children's height and the fact that they were chest high to the adult (SAO-2791).

6:30 p.m. (sometime after): Charles Ridulph (Maria's brother) and a friend were in the den of the Ridulph home when Maria entered the house in search of a doll to show "Johnny." SA Schmack notes here that it was several minutes after Randy had come over to listen to records with Chuck, which would put it sometime after 6:30 p.m. (SAO-2722).

6:40 p.m. (about): Frances Ridulph saw Maria enter the downstairs bedroom where she was reading a newspaper. Frances asks Maria what she was looking for. Maria stated she wanted her new doll to take outside and show someone. Frances told her to take an older doll as she didn't want Maria's new doll to get dirty (SAO-2704, 2710, 2729).

6:30 to 6:45 p.m. (approximately): Michael Ridulph (Maria's father) saw Maria enter the living room and rummage for a doll in the corner where her toys were kept. Michael was watching "Cheyenne" on TV when Maria entered, picked a doll, and left. The "Cheyenne" episode started at 6:30 p.m. according to local programming at that time (SAO-2710). On December 4, 1957, Mr. Ridulph told Winnebago County deputies Iasparro and Ferona he saw

Kathy waiting outside for Maria several feet from the door (SAO-2729). On December 15, Mr. Ridulph told the FBI that Kathy was not waiting at the door when Maria was home getting her doll, admitting that he was so engrossed in "Cheyenne" that he barely noticed Maria when she came into the room (SAO-2714).

6:40 p.m. (about): Larry Wilkins saw Kathy and Maria walking east under the streetlight on Archie Place toward Maria's house. The FBI confirmed visibility of the sidewalk under the streetlight in front of 631 Archie Place (mid-block) from the Wilkins' back yard (SAO-2783, 2784, 2816). (Note: This observation conflicts with Kathy's account of events that evening. According to Kathy, she remained on the corner with Johnny while Maria went home to get a doll.)

6:45 to 6:50 p.m. (about): Maria returned to the corner with her doll. Johnny admired the doll, and then gave Maria another brief piggyback ride. Kathy then asked Johnny for the time and he said it was 7 p.m. Kathy said her hands were cold and told "Johnny" she was going home to get her mittens. Before leaving the corner, Kathy asked Maria to come with her. Maria refused and stayed on the corner with Johnny (SAO-2980, 3000).

6:45 p.m. (about): Shirley Niewold, 506 Center Cross (which is directly across from the corner), stood in the front doorway as she waited for her brother, John, to pull his car around to pick her up and take her to Teentown. She said she waited there several minutes for her brother. As John pulled his car out of the driveway, his headlights were shining directly at the corner. Neither Shirley nor John Niewold saw the girls or anyone else on the corner (SAO-2808).

6:45 to 7 p.m.: Time of Maria's disappearance according to Chief Hindenburg. Info passed to Joliet Police while discussing a potential suspect on May 12, 1958 (SAO-631).

6:50 to 6:55 p.m. (about): Larry Wilkins saw Kathy walking beneath the streetlight on Archie, headed toward her home (SAO-2783, 2784, 2816). (Note: The Taylor kids' mother was interviewed and said her kids didn't see anything. There are no reports of interviews with the Taylor kids (SAO-2818).)

6:50 to 6:55 p.m.: Kathy entered her home, got her mittens, and asked her mother, Flora Sigman, if she could go back outside to continue playing with Maria. Flora gave Kathy her permission. Kathy ran back to the corner of Archie Place and Center Cross Street. Maria and Johnny were gone. Kathy's brother, Carl Edward, left the home to join the girls in play at the corner (SAO-2981, 2704).

6:55 p.m. (about): Kathy looked up and down the street, calling out Maria's name, saying, "This isn't funny." She then went to the Ridulph house to see if Maria had gone inside. Chuck answered the door and told her Maria was still outside. He told Kathy to look outside for her. (Frances Ridulph estimated the time as 6:45 p.m. when Kathy came to their door to ask about Maria, but Flora Sigman gave the time of Kathy's arrival at home as about 6:50 or 6:55 p.m. This seems like a reasonable time, as Maria first retrieved her doll at 6:40 p.m., then went out, showed the doll to her abductor, got a piggyback ride, and then Kathy left to get her mittens. It is reasonable to estimate the time of Kathy's return to the corner was about 6:55 p.m. at the earliest, based on Mr. Strombom having seen Mr. Ridulph on the porch yelling for Maria as he left his home to go back to work at 6:58 p.m. (very accurate estimate given by Mrs. Strombom based on "Name That Tune" having just ended. Mr. Strombom put the time at 6:55 p.m.). These estimates could move up the time of Maria's abduction by a few minutes—perhaps five— depending upon how much time Kathy spent searching at the corner (SAO-2981).

6:55 to 7 p.m.: Kathy and her brother, Carl Edward, who had joined her by then, returned to the Ridulph home after a second search at the corner. Kathy told Chuck Maria could not be found (SAO-2981).

6:57 to 6:59 p.m.: In Rockford, IL, about 42 miles away from Sycamore, John Tessier made a collect call from a phone booth located in the lobby of the post office, 401 S. Main Street, to his stepfather, Ralph Tessier, asking for a ride home (SAO-3154).

6:58 p.m. (accurate): David Strombom left home to return to his work as sales manager at Fargo Motors, 427 W. State Street. As he exited, he saw and heard Mr. Ridulph come out the side door of his house and call for Maria. Mrs. Strombom was very confident of the time because the TV show "Name That Tune" had just ended. Two minutes is a good estimate for the time between the end of one TV show and the start of the next, allowing for a short commercial break, return for the rolling credits of the show that just ended, station identification, a short ID by the local affiliate, a short aural tone marking the top of the hour (7 p.m. in this case), and then the start of the next show (SAO-756, 2669, 2793).

7 p.m. (about): Mr. Ridulph went back inside to get his police whistle. As he went back outside, he blew it as a way to call for Maria. He saw Kathy and Carl Edward in his driveway (SAO-2710). Mr. and Mrs. Ridulph searched at the corner, and then searched their yard. Mrs. Ridulph went across the street to the Lindstroms, 625 Archie, to see if Maria had gone there. Next, Mr. and Mrs. Ridulph got into their car and drove up to Roosevelt Court to look for Maria at the Peterson home at 615 Roosevelt. Johnny Peterson was a regular playmate to both Maria and Kathy (SAO-2712).

7 p.m.: Two neighbors, Elmer Westburg and Mrs. Stanley (Barbara) Wells, heard a girl scream or a screech (SAO-2781 & SAO-2792). (Note: If Johnny and Maria made their way through the back lots toward Fair Street, then what Mrs. Wells and Mr. Westburg heard was more likely Mr. Ridulph blowing his whistle, or else why wouldn't anyone to the west on Archie, DeKalb Avenue, or Fair Street have also reported hearing the scream?) (SAO-2790, 2681, 2779).

7:05 p.m. (about): Kathy and Carl Edward arrived home and informed their mother that Maria was lost. Mrs. Sigman sent them back out to look for Maria. (SAO2981)

7:10 to 7:15 p.m. (about): Mike and Frances Ridulph were on Roosevelt Court outside the Peterson home blowing the police whistle and calling for Maria. From there, they drove around the block, meeting Chuck, Pat, and Randy near DeKalb Avenue and Fair Street, and proceeded back to their home (SAO-2705, 2712).

7:15 to 7:30 p.m. (about): John Tessier encountered Col. Liebovich and Sgt. Froom, who describe Tessier as looking like "a lost sheep" at the Rockford Post Office (SAO-3076). He left paperwork that he had been given earlier that day at the induction center with Froom. This is the paperwork John went over with Sgt. Oswald on the following morning, December 4. (SAO-3076, 3077).

7 to 7:30 p.m. (sometime between): Paul Holderness arrived at the Ridulph home looking for Kay. Mr. Ridulph told him Kay was not home (SAO-2714). This is likely after 7:20 p.m., as Mr. Ridulph was home alone at this time. Kay had not yet come home from her voice lesson. Chuck and Randy, along with Pat, left about 7:20 p.m. with Mrs. Strombom's permission to search the neighborhood.

7:20 p.m. (about): Neighbors were coming out to search for Maria after Mrs. Ridulph went to the Lindstrom house, 625 Archie Place, across the street, looking for Maria (SAO-2705).

7:20 p.m. (about): Mrs. Strombom gave permission to Chuck and Randy Strombom to search the neighborhood for Maria. Pat joined them (SAO-2725-C, 2793, 2794-R). (This time doesn't mesh with Mr. and Mrs. Ridulph driving around the block at 7:10 to 7:15 p.m. and picking up the kids near DeKalb and Fair.)

7:25 p.m. (about): Kay, after walking home from her voice lesson, arrived and found out that Maria was missing (SAO-2705).

7:30 p.m. (about): Kay went to the Sigman house to talk with Kathy. She was joined by Chuck and Randy. There, they got the story of Johnny from Kathy, including Kathy saying that Johnny "talked like we used to," which Kay assumed she meant Johnny talked like a hillbilly (SAO-2723). Mrs. Sigman told Kay that Kathy was confused about her stories of what happened and of her description of Johnny (SAO-742).

7:30 p.m. (about): John Boies of 303 Center Cross returned home from walking the dog. He told his family that Maria was missing and the Ridulphs were looking for her (SAO-2752). Shortly afterward, Chuck and Randy stopped at the Boies house looking for Maria.

7:45 to 8 p.m.: Tom Braddy, 121 Fair Street, got a call from either Mr. or Mrs. Cliffe, who told him the Ridulphs were looking for their daughter, Maria (SAO-2781). In July of 1958, Braddy told ISP Troopers Fraher and Bales he got this phone call from Mrs. Cliffe at no later than 7:10 p.m. (SAO-741) This time makes no sense, as will be pointed out below.

7:50 p.m. (about): Mrs. Ridulph and daughter Pat set out for the police station to report Maria missing (SAO-2706). They drove by a creek on Mill Street and a lumberyard on Grant Street on the off chance that Maria might be playing there. At about 8 p.m., they arrived at the police station and informed the Sycamore Police about Maria's disappearance (SAO-2706).

8 p.m. (or sometime before): The snow stopped falling and the clouds began to clear, allowing a waxing moon, 85 percent full, to help light up the area. This was made brighter still by the moonlight reflecting back up off the new fallen snow (the albedo effect). This helped the search team, headed by Tom Braddy, as they followed footprints in the snow through the back lots. (SAO-2788).

8:10 to 8:15 p.m.: Tom Braddy and his 19-year-old son, Dale, went to help in the search. At the corner they met Bud Sigman, Kathy's father, and Sycamore PD Officer Singer, who had just arrived on the scene (likely the first to respond to Chief Hindenburg's call). This puts the start of Braddy's search too late for the 7:10 p.m. phone call he told the ISP in July of 1958. The four of them found the footprints in the snow of an adult and a child walking side-by-side next to Ida Johnson's garage and through the back lots behind houses on Archie leading toward Fair Street. The prints were so fresh that the group separated and circled the garage from opposite sides believing the kidnapper and Maria might be behind the garage. During their search, Dale Braddy compared his shoe size with the adult's footprints. He estimated the adult wore a shoe size 8, based on his own shoe size being 9 (SAO-2786 to 2789).

8:10 p.m.: Chief Hindenburg sent the message out over the radio about Maria being missing. (SAO-15).

8:15 p.m. (about): Mike Ridulph arrived at the police station in the Ridulphs' second car, and was joined later by Kay, who had walked. He told the police that Johnny talked like a hillbilly, relaying the info Kay had brought home from the Sigman house after talking with Kathy. He had just missed Frances and Pat (SAO-2712).

8:20 p.m. (about): Tom and Dale Braddy went home to get warmer clothes. They returned a few minutes later, joined by Braddy's 17-year-old daughter, Joy. He spoke to

Mr. Ridulph in the Ridulph's front yard, and then restarted his search in the back lots, where he once again found the footprints in the snow (SAO-2788).

8:25 p.m. (about): Chief Hindenburg arrived at Archie and Center Cross. Shortly afterward, he went to the Sigman home to speak with Kathy. (Schmack has this in his exhibits, March 25, 2016. He did not provide a reference.)

9 p.m. (or a little before): During the search, Maria's doll was discovered by Mrs. Strombom lying on the ground near a rock near the northeast corner of Ida Johnson's garage. She was searching with Mrs. Cliffe, Pat, and Kay. When Pat and Kay saw the doll, they recognized it as Maria's, screamed, and ran home. Several others had previously searched the area without finding the doll (SAO-2717, 2790, 2978). Mrs. Strombom said this was between 8 and 9 p.m. However, Mrs. Ridulph puts it at 9 p.m.

9:30 p.m. (about): Louis Salemi dropped his girlfriend, Jane Niewold, off at her home at 506 Center Cross after an evening at Teentown. He learned about Maria's disappearance and joined the search (SAO-2802). By now, there were hundreds of people who had joined the search in the neighborhood.

10:20 p.m. (about): The Illinois State Police are informed that Maria is missing (SAO-2790).

10:30 p.m. (about): Roadblocks are established by the ISP, and police begin searching vehicles moving in and out of Sycamore (Rockford Register Star, December 5, 1957, SAO-2312, 2314).

11 p.m. (about): Thomas Followell, 937 Esther, first heard loudspeakers (SAO-2783).

A list of people who drove past or near the corner at around the crucial time, 6 to 7 p.m., and what they reported:

- **6 p.m.:** Sycamore resident Fred Scott said he saw an old black car parked at the corner (SAO-591). It is possible he saw Tom Braddy's truck.

- **6 p.m.:** Tom Moore, 203½ Center Cross, saw Tom Braddy's truck at the corner (SAO-591).

- **6:10 p.m. (about):** Mrs. Edith Taylor and her kids passed the corner on their way to the Wilkins home at 628 Roosevelt Court. They saw nothing at the corner, not even Braddy's truck (SAO-2818).

- **6:30 p.m. (about):** Aaron Malm, 438½ State St., went bowling in DeKalb. He passed the corner, but didn't see the girls. He saw a "farm truck" parked about 50 to 75 feet from the corner (SAO-2797). On May 14, 1958, Malm told the ISP he saw a "two-ton truck" parked near Ridulph residence sometime between 6:25 and 6:35 p.m. (SAO-675).

- **6:30 p.m.:** John Merchant drove west on DeKalb Avenue and stopped at the stop sign at Center Cross. He looked closely for cars and pedestrians coming down Center Cross, but saw nothing. This was a short block away from the corner where the girls were playing (SAO-2818).

- **6:50 p.m. (about):** Mr. and Mrs. Mattingly passed the corner and saw an older model (1949) Chrysler parked adjacent to the Cliffes', pointed south, a few feet north of Ida Johnson's driveway (SAO-2810, 2811). On May 14, 1958, she told the ISP it was about 6:40 p.m. (SAO-674).

- **6:50 p.m. (approximate time of kidnapping):** Mrs. Ralph (Vivian) Wells, 327 Center Cross, reported seeing William Crego's truck in the area. She knew Crego and knew he had spent time in Stateville prison for attempted molestation of his 13-year-old babysitter (SAO-1388).

· **6:50 p.m. (approximate time of kidnapping):** Gordon McDaniel of Malta, IL, was driving home from his work as an equipment operator on the Illinois Toll Road near Franklin Park. As he turned south onto Center Cross, he saw a car stopped in the southbound lane about two car lengths south of Archie. He drove down Center Cross and came up behind the car, still waiting to make a lefthand turn. It finally turned into the driveway at 506 Center Cross (the Niewold home). Traffic was heavy and the car had to wait a long time. The car was a 1955 or 56 Ford convertible (SAO-2804). This was almost certainly 16-year-old John Niewold coming home after taking his 15-year-old sister Shirley to Teentown, having left his home at about 6:45 p.m.

EPILOGUE

Days after a DeKalb County judge declared him innocent in the 1957 kidnapping and murder of Maria Ridulph, in January 2017, Jack McCullough filed suit against state and local authorities accusing them of framing him.

McCullough's wrongful conviction lawsuit, filed in federal court in Rockford, accuses Sycamore, state and Seattle police of conspiring with DeKalb County prosecutors to frame McCullough attorney, Russell

Ainsworth, said the quick turnaround was essential. "It's been a year since Jack was released from prison, and we wanted to get justice for Jack," said Ainsworth, a Chicago-based attorney with the civil rights firm Lovey & Lovey. "He's 77 years old. He can't wait forever."

The suit names 15 defendants, including DeKalb County, the city of Sycamore, former DeKalb County state's attorney Clay Campbell and assistant state's attorneys Victor Escarcida and Julie Treva, Sycamore police officers Daniel Hoffman and Tiffany Ziegler, as well as Illinois State Police Detective Brion Hanley, who was named the Illinois State Police's "Officer of the Year" in 2013 for his work as lead investigator on the case. It also names Seattle police detectives and the city of Seattle. It seeks unspecified compensatory damages and attorney's fees.

"Although exonerated, Mr. McCullough must now attempt to resume his life despite the horrors he endured while imprisoned for a crime he did not commit," the lawsuit states. "Plaintiff was due to retire, but those efforts have been hampered by his wrongful conviction. In addition, Plaintiff has lost the precious time to be with his family, and watch his grandchildren age—something he can never get back."

McCullough accuses police and prosecutors of fabricating evidence. He says they created a false timeline for the crime in order to explain away the fact that he placed a collect call from Rockford to his home at 6:57 p.m. the night Maria disappeared. He says they created a biased photo lineup leading to false identification by the only witness to the crime, Kathy Sigman, who was playing with Maria the night she was abducted near the intersection of Center Cross and Archie Place. He claims they withheld evidence of McCullough's innocence and ignored the fact that the FBI had ruled McCullough out as a suspect in its initial investigation in the 1950s.

McCullough says Hanley and others sought false testimony from jailhouse informants in exchange for favors, and then told them to lie about the arrangement.

The suit claims the prosecution, under then-state's attorney Clay Campbell, did all this to gain fame and fast-track careers by securing a conviction in the case 55 years after the crime. Authorities have stated they can't comment on matters in litigation. Campbell said a successful lawsuit of this sort typically brings the plaintiff $1 million to $2 million for each year of imprisonment, but he claims McCullough's circumstances make his as unique. "We're talking about justice for a man ripped from his home and being put in prison, where he very well could have died," Ainsworth said.

McCullough, who was transferred from DeKalb County custody to the Menard Correctional Center after he was sentenced to life in prison, was stabbed in the eye by a cellmate while he slept, the suit says. He was freed in April 2016, after former DeKalb County state's attorney Richard Schmack, relying on FBI reports about the crime and having located records that showed the phone that McCullough was believed to have called from was in the downtown Rockford post office, concluded McCullough was in Rockford at the time of Ridulph's disappearance and couldn't have committed the crime.

On July 21, 2016, Casey Porter, son-in-law to McCullough, filed a lawsuit in Cook County, Illinois, against the Illinois State Police and Sycamore Police Department for refusal to comply with a Freedom of Information Act request related to the investigation of the case. McCullough filed a lawsuit April 15, 2017, against DeKalb County, the city of Sycamore, police officers, former DeKalb County officials and the city of Seattle for his wrongful conviction, accusing authorities of framing him.

188 | ALAN R. WARREN

ABOUT THE AUTHOR

Alan R. Warren is one of the hosts of the popular True Crime Radio Show called "House of Mystery" heard on KKNW 1150 A.M. in Seattle, Washington, on Fridays at 4 p.m. The show is now syndicated throughout the United States and Canada including KFNX 1150 AM Phoenix, KYAH 540 AM in Salt Lake City, Utah Mondays to Fridays at 8 a.m. and 4 p.m. as well as on KCAA 106.5 FM Los Angeles/Riverside/ Palm Springs Mondays to Fridays 1 a.m.

He is also the best-selling author of six true crime books and is a contributing writer for True Crime Case Files Magazine and Serial Killer Magazine.

Alan received his Recording & Sound Engineering degree from the Juno Award-winning Bullfrog Studios in Vancouver, B.C. Canada, Certificate in Business from BCIT, Vancouver, Masters Music Degree in Music with a minor in Criminology at the University of Washington, Seattle.

SOURCES

1. Jack Daniel McCullough – personal interview

2. Casey Porter – personal interview and the information that he had collected for his website called "Last Man Standing." Located on the internet at https://jackdmccullough.wordpress.com/

3. "You Don't Know Jack" – book written and self-published by Jack McCullough, August 31, 2017 – Jack McCullough ISBN:1975960599

4. Charles Lachman – Interview #1 Episode #19 – 2015 and #2 on House of Mystery KFNX 100 AM Phoenix episode #3 2015

5. Jeffrey Doty – Interview #1 episode #19 – House of Mystery on KFNX 1100 AM Phoenix 2015

6. "Footsteps in the Snow" – written by Charles Lachman – Publisher Berkley 2014 ISBN: 0425272885

7. "Footsteps in the Snow" – Lifetime movie, November 12, 2014

8. Dr. Phillip McGraw – "Dr. Phil" show October 14, 2014, "Cold Case Murder of Maria Ridulph"

9. FBI case papers 1957-1958

10. Sycamore Police file – 1957-1968

11. Seattle Police Department records of investigation – 1978 and 2012

12. "Dr. Phil" show November 4, 2014 – Telling body language of Jack McCullough

13. "48 Hours" episode, "Cold as Ice," March 9, 2013

14. Erin Moriarty, CBS news, "Teen's diary offers account of sister's 1957 disappearance, murder," March 9, 2013

15. "Unspoken Truth A Memoir of Abuse" – written by Jeanne Marie Tessier – 2009 self-published pdf.

16. Dailey Chronical July 13, 2007 – news @ shaemedia.com

17. American Bar Association, November 1, 2017

18. North West Harold – August 23, 2016 – Eric R. Olson, Brett Rowland – State's attorney investigates perjury in Ridulph case

CHAPTER 1

YESTERDAY, WHEN I WAS YOUNG

Rodney Alcala was born Rodrigo (Rodney) Jacques Alcala Buquor in San Antonio, Texas, to Raoul Alcala Buquor and Maria Gutierrez on August 23, 1943, where he lived with his three siblings, parents, and his maternal grandmother. Raoul, born in 1941, was the oldest; Marie Therese, born in

1942, was next; then came Rodney; and then younger sister Maria Christine, who was born in 1947.

They lived in an average middle-class neighborhood in a four-bedroom home near the Alamo and the San Antonio city zoo. Rodney had his own bedroom, and the sisters had to share one bedroom. The kids all attended either public or private Catholic schools in their elementary years, as their religious faith was very important to their mother. Rodney was known as an excellent student. Throughout his school years, he consistently had excellent grades and above-average intelligence. There were never any reports by the school that Alcala ever caused any trouble.

In 1951, his grandmother became ill and the prognosis was not good. After many discussions with the family, it was decided that they all would move back to Mexico, so that she could live out the rest of her life in the home where she was raised, as well as be with her family.

After moving back down to Mexico, the children got to attend regular schools without the religious teachings. The girls really enjoyed it, as they didn't have to wear a uniform. It was only a couple of years before their grandmother died, and their father then abandoned them in Mexico to move back to the States.

Three years later, his mother moved Rodney, who was about 11 years old at the time, and his siblings to suburban Los Angeles. In 1960, Rodney graduated from high school at the top of his class. He was very popular among the girls at school and always seemed to have dates.

In 1961, he then joined the US Army in North Carolina to become a paratrooper and worked as a clerk, following his brother's lead, who was at West Point. He was only in the army about one year when his father died suddenly. Even though his father was remarried, the family remained close, and they all attended his funeral service. Rodney returned to North Carolina after the funeral and continued in the service.

About a year later, in 1963, Rodney suddenly turned up at home while his mother was cooking dinner one night. She was shocked and when she asked Rodney what he was doing home, he told her that he had hitchhiked home and gone AWOL. She was frantic and urged him to turn himself in. He had to, he didn't want to wreck his life and all his hard work to get where he was. A few days later, he went into the local army detachment and turned himself in. He was interviewed by several different officers and eventually sent to an army psychologist, who hospitalized him and told him he needed urgent psychological care. When the hospital checked with Rodney's superior officers back in Fort Bragg, North Carolina, they learned that in the last few weeks before he went AWOL, Rodney was unable to perform his duties and was suffering from a type of nervous breakdown. Rodney was diagnosed with antisocial personality disorder by a military psychiatrist and discharged on medical grounds.

CHAPTER 2

GOOD SAMARITAN (TALI SHAPIRO; 1968)

Alcala committed his first known crime on September 25, 1968, when a motorist in Los Angeles called police after watching him lure an eight-year-old girl named Tali Shapiro into his Hollywood apartment.

Tali was walking down Sunset Boulevard on her way to her school, Gardner Elementary. Tali was new to this area of West Hollywood, as her home had burned down recently, so

Tali and her family were now staying at the famous Chateau Marmont Hotel.

This was one of the most luxurious hotels on the strip, with beautiful large bedrooms with plush carpeting and formal dining rooms. Each suite had large balconies that overlooked the lights and action of Hollywood. The Marmont also offered their guests an outdoor swimming pool, gorgeous gardens, and a grand reception lobby; the perfect setting for all the Hollywood stars.

As far back as the 1930s, everybody from Greta Garbo and Bette Davis to John Wayne and Marilyn Monroe were regular faces at the hotel. Now in the 60s, rock stars started to frequent the hotel as it was known as the place to go for discretion; back then, bad rumors could ruin your career. This was the place that Jim Morrison from The Doors jumped off his suite balcony, and Bonzo from Led Zeppelin drove his motorbike into the lobby of the hotel.

As Rodney Alcala drove down the strip, he noticed eight-year-old Tali skipping down the sidewalk and singing. He slowed his car to a crawl and yelled out to her, "Hey, sunshine, do you need a ride?"

Tali was startled and almost tripped as she stopped to see who it was that was talking to her. She looked around to see Rodney halfway standing in his convertible car and smiling intently at her. "Do you need a ride somewhere?" he asked again.

"I'm going to school now," Tali said.

"That's okay, I'll take you there, get in!" Alcala exclaimed.

"Do you know where I go to school?" she asked him.

"Why, sure I do; get in, I'll take you there." Alcala then grinned widely. He knelt over with his right knee on the passenger seat and opened up the passenger side door from inside the car. Tali smiled as well, helped open up the car door, and quickly hopped onto the passenger seat.

As Rodney reached over Tali to close the passenger side door, he could smell some sort of a flower scent on her, and as he closed the door shut, he asked, "What is that lovely smell?" Tali looked up and her eyes met his. She was confused by the question, as she wasn't wearing any sort of perfume or anything, so she stuttered, not knowing what to say.

As Alcala took his seat and put the car in drive, he turned and said that she smelled like a lovely flower.

Tali started to sing again as the car drove down the road. It was a short while after that Alcala had pulled into what looked like a hotel or apartment building and parked.

"This isn't my school," Tali said.

"Oh, I know that. I need to get something from my apartment first, is that okay?" Alcala asked.

"I don't want to be late," she replied. "I will get in trouble."

"Don't worry about that. I will come with you into the school and tell your teacher that it was my fault, okay?"

"Okay."

Rodney got out of his car and shut his car door. "Do you want to come with me?"

Tali got really quiet, looked down at her feet in the car, and replied, "I don't know."

"Oh, come on, I have some candy that you can have, and we will only be a minute."

He grinned again as he walked over to the passenger side of the car, and opened her door. She got out of the car carefully and stood out of the way as he closed the door. Rodney took her hand and walked her up the three flights of stairs, unlocked his apartment door, and walked in the apartment with her.

"I was out doing my patrols. We just started our shift that day. I was driving down Sunset Boulevard and I had received a call," Los Angeles Police Officer Chris Camacho recalls of that September morning in 1968.

"A beige-colored car with no license plates was following this little girl," says Orange County Deputy District Attorney Matt Murphy.

"A good Samaritan, Donald Haines, a witness, sees the little girl, the little eight-year-old Tali, get in the car. Thinks it's suspicious and follows him, and puts a call into LAPD from a payphone," says Los Angeles Detective Steve Hodel.

"I went to that location," Camacho recalls, "and I started knocking. I said 'Police officer. Open the door. I need to talk to you.' This male appeared at the door. I will always remember that face at that door, very evil face. And he says, 'I'm in the shower. I gotta get dressed.' I told him 'OK. You got ten seconds. Open this door, I want to talk to you.' Finally, I kicked the door in. The image will be with me forever. We could see in the kitchen there was a body on the floor, a lot of blood."

"They say a picture says a thousand words," Murphy says, "and that image of those little white Mary Janes (classic Mary Janes for children are typically made of black leather or patent leather, have one thin strap fastened with a buckle or button abroad, and rounded toe box, low heels, and thin outsoles) on that floor with that metal bar that he used to strangle her with, and that puddle of blood, it just looked like too much blood to come out of a tiny little eight year old like that."

"She had been raped. There was no breathing and I thought she was dead. We all thought she was dead," Camacho recalls. "So, I grabbed a towel and I picked up the edge of the bar and I laid it off to the side. We started searching the residence and there was a lot of photography equipment,"

Camacho continues. "All of us were amazed at the number of photographs he had there of young girls, very young girls. We found a lot of ID, a picture ID of a Rodney Alcala. He was a student at UCLA, an undergrad student."

That was one of the first times he ever turned up on the radar for law enforcement, but Rodney Alcala managed to give them the slip.

"Unfortunately," Camacho explains, "the other officers, when I kicked the front door came running around to assist me and the suspect went out the back door." But moments later, when Camacho walked back into the kitchen where Tali was, he witnessed a miracle. "She was gagging and trying to breathe. And I thought, 'One for the good guys.' She's going to make it."

Clinging to life, Tali was rushed to the hospital.

"Had it not been for that police officer, Tali Shapiro would have died on Rodney Alcala's kitchen floor," says Orange County Deputy DA Matt Murphy.

"When I was in Vietnam and we were in combat, I was trying to save this guy, and didn't do it. He died. So, with Tali, it was kind of like God gave me a second chance to save someone," says Camacho.

Soon after Tali healed, her parents moved her out of the country. "I found out that they had moved to Mexico, that they did not want to raise their daughter in this society any longer. And that was the last I heard of them," says Camacho.

http://wbp.bz/tkga

SAVING ANNIE: A TRUE STORY by STEVE JACKSON

http://wbp.bz/savingannie1

Read A Sample Next

CHAPTER ONE

March 16, 2009

Hood River County, Oregon

6:09 p.m.

When the 911 call came into the Hood River Sheriff's Office, it wasn't so much what the caller said, but how he said it.

His voice neither rose nor fell as he phlegmatically relayed the information.

911 OPERATOR: *"911, where is your emergency?*

CALLER: *"Hello. I need help. I'm at, uh, Eagle Creek."*

911 OPERATOR: *"Okay, and what's going on there?"*

CALLER: *"My girlfriend fell off the cliff. I hiked back. And I'm in my car."*

911 OPERATOR: *"Okay. You're at the Eagle Creek Trailhead right now?"*

CALLER: *"Yeah."*

911 OPERATOR: *"Okay, and where on the trail did she fall?"*

CALLER: *"I don't know. I think about a mile up."*

911 OPERATOR: *"Okay."*

The 911 operator thought it was odd. That he was odd. Normally people calling 911 to report a traumatic event are in an agitated state with an emotional element in their speech ranging from weeping to a rapid-fire data dump to shouting or screaming. This guy might as well have been reading a manual on how to change a sparkplug.

CALLER: *"I hiked down and got her, uh, and I'm in my car now, and I don't know if I ... (unintelligible)"*

911 OPERATOR: *"Okay."*

CALLER: *"... suffering from hypothermia. I don't think it's that cold but ..."*

911 OPERATOR: *"Okay, so she fell off the trail down a cliff, and then you went down the cliff and pulled her, brought her back up onto the trail?"*

CALLER: *"No she's dead."*

There was a stunned pause as the operator absorbed his last statement; 911 callers in emergency situations tend to get to the point right away and gush with information. But this was more worried about telling her in his flat, monotone voice that he was cold than that his girlfriend had just died. And every time the operator tried to get more details about the victim, he turned the conversation back to his needs.

CALLER: *"I went down to get her. I went to the bottom. Then in the river (unintelligible) took me about an hour to get to her. I finally go over to her, then I was startin' to shake. I got too cold, so I'm, uh, now, I just got to my car, and I need someone to come and help me ... Please send someone I'm at, uh ..."*

911 OPERATOR: *"Okay, hang on just a minute ..."*

CALLER: *"... Eagle Creek."*

911 OPERATOR: *"... one second."*

CALLER: *"Okay."*

911 OPERATOR: *"And what's, what's your name, sir?"*

CALLER: *"Steve."*

911 OPERATOR: *"Okay Steve, what is, um ..."*

CALLER: *"I'm freezing. Will you please send someone?"*

911 OPERATOR: *"Um, hang on just one second for me, okay?"*

CALLER: *"All right."*

911 OPERATOR: *"Steve, what is your last name?"*

CALLER: *"Nichols."*

911 OPERATOR: *"And what's her name, Steve?"*

CALLER: *"Rhonda."*

911 OPERATOR: *"Rhonda's last name?"*

CALLER: *"Casto."*

911 OPERATOR: *"Could you spell that for me please?"*

CALLER: *"R-H-O-N-D-A ... C-A-S-T-O."*

911 OPERATOR: *"Do you need an ambulance? Do you feel like you might need medical attention?"*

CALLER: *"I don't know if I'm shaking from, I don't know … I'm really cold."*

911 OPERATOR: *"Okay, okay, Steve."*

CALLER: *"I'm just really cold."*

911 OPERATOR: *"Are you able to start the car and get warm?"*

CALLER: *"Yeah, the …"*

911 OPERATOR: *"Blankets?"*

CALLER: *"… car is running."*

911 OPERATOR: *"And now Steve, I know this is a difficult question for you to answer for me, but what makes you think she was deceased?"*

CALLER: *"I don't know it for sure. I stayed with her for about an hour and a half, and I gave her mouth-to-mouth, and I tried covering up her leg. There was blood coming out of her leg, and I just sat and helped her, and then I started shaking uncontrollably, so …* (unintelligible)*"*

911 OPERATOR: *"Okay."*

CALLER: *"Had to go back, and …"*

911 OPERATOR: *"Was she breathing when you left her?"*

CALLER: *"No."*

911 OPERATOR: *"Do you know if she had a pulse?"*

CALLER: *"Uh, no, I don't think so."*

911 OPERATOR: *"Okay, Steve, we have an officer who's on his way."*

CALLER: *"All right. How long … how long will it take an ambulance to get here?"*

911 OPERATOR: *"It'll take just a minute. Would you like an ambulance for you?"*

CALLER: *"Uh, uh ..."*

911 OPERATOR: *"If there's a question, I can send them, and, um, then you can decide not to go with them if that's what you choose to do."*

CALLER: *"Just so cold. That's the thing, I'm cold. ... How long will it take to the police car to get here?"*

911 OPERATOR: *"They're on their way, okay? Hang on just a second. How far down the trail, how far over the cliff is she?"*

CALLER: *"Uh, I don't know, like a hundred feet ..."*

911 OPERATOR: *"A hundred feet, okay."*

CALLER: *"I don't know."*

911 OPERATOR: *"Steve, how old are you?"*

CALLER: *"Uh, 34."*

911 OPERATOR: *"I'm going to send the ambulance for you, okay?"*

CALLER: *"All right."*

911 OPERATOR: *"Hang on just a second for me. You're going to hear some silence, okay?"*

CALLER: *"Okay."*

The caller waited patiently and quietly for the 911 operator to get back on the line. When she did, she assured him that the ambulance was on its way and she would stay on the line with him until somebody got there.

CALLER: *" 'kay."*

911 OPERATOR: *"And we have an officer on his way from Hood River."*

CALLER: *"Where's that?"*

911 OPERATOR: *"Hood River? Um, it's about twenty minutes away, but he's on his way, about seven minutes ago, okay, and we have an officer coming from Corbett. Do you know where that's at?"*

CALLER: *"No I don't."*

911 OPERATOR: *"He's a little closer so he'll be there shortly."*

CALLER: *"Okay."*

911 OPERATOR: *"So I'm going to stay on the phone with you. Are you getting any warmer in the vehicle with the heat on, Steve?"*

CALLER: *"No but I have it on full so that should heat up."*

911 OPERATOR: *"Are you in wet clothes at all?"*

CALLER: *"Tried to ... (unintelligible) ... up river. Uh, was too strong, so ..."*

911 OPERATOR: *"Are you able to get your wet clothes off and put something else warmer on?"*

CALLER: *"Yeah ... (unintelligible) ... shirt off."*

911 OPERATOR: *"You what? You have warmer clothes to put on or dry clothes at least?*

The caller was silent.

911 CALLER: *"Steve?*

Still no answer.

911 OPERATOR: *"... Steve? ... Steve?"*

CALLER: *"Yeah, that helps. ... How far away is he?"*

911 OPERATOR: *"He said just a few minutes."*

CALLER: *"Okay."*

911 OPERATOR: *"Are you there?"*

CALLER: *"Yeah."*

911 OPERATOR: *"Hang on just a second for me, okay?"*

There were several more pauses over the next couple of minutes as the operator checked with law enforcement and the ambulance crew. Again, the caller patiently waited for her return and would then inquire as to when someone would be there to help him. He never once said anything about his girlfriend without being asked a direct question.

CALLER: *"What time is it?"*

911 OPERATOR: *"It's 6:18. They're going to be there in a few minutes, okay?"*

CALLER: *"Okay."*

911 OPERATOR: *"So Steve, how far up the trail did you say she is?"*

CALLER: *"I don't know. I think a mile."*

911 OPERATOR: *"Okay. What was she wearing?"*

CALLER: *"Uh, jeans. ... I don't know the top. ... She put on my shirt, but I think she put one over ..."*

911 OPERATOR: *"Okay. They're on their way, okay?"*

CALLER: *"Yeah."*

911 OPERATOR: *"Hang on one second for me, Steve, okay?"*

CALLER: *"Mm hmm."*

The 911 OPERATOR spoke to one of the responding officers: *"Brandon ... (unintelligible) ... responding? I have a hypothermic guy sitting in his car."*

The 911 OPERATOR then addressed the caller. *"They're on their way, okay."*

THE CALLER: *"Uh huh."*

911 OPERATOR: *"They're on their way. They said less than five minutes, okay? He'll be there in just a couple of minutes."*

THE CALLER: *"All right."*

The operator asked a few more perfunctory questions, such as date of birth for both the caller, January 4, 1975, and his girlfriend, July 2, 1985. The operator then attempted to gather more details about the "accident."

911 OPERATOR: *"Do you know what made her fall, Steve? Did she lose her footing, or did she get hurt? ... Do you know why she fell?"*

CALLER: *"I think she's high on something."*

911 OPERATOR: *"Have you done any drugs or alcohol today?"*

CALLER: *"No."*

911 OPERATOR: *"What do you think she's high on?"*

CALLER: *"I don't know. She always hides that stuff from me."*

911 OPERATOR: *"Okay. Are you doing okay?"*

CALLER: *"Yeah, I'm warming up a little."*

911 OPERATOR: *"Oh, you're ..."*

CALLER: *"Shaking. ... I can't stop shaking."*

911 OPERATOR: *"The ambulance is on its way. It will be there in a few minutes."*

CALLER: *"Uh huh."*

Again the 911 OPERATOR broke to speak to the responding officers: *"Are you guys aware of what's going on?"* After speaking to them, she returned to the CALLER: *"Did you leave anything on the trail showing where she went down over the cliff? ... Did you leave a backpack or anything there?"*

CALLER: *"No, I left my backpack ... (unintelligible) ... farther down, so I could go down. But then when I made my way back up, I got it. ... Only thing I left was my sweatshirt."*

911 OPERATOR: *"You left your sweatshirt there on the trail?"*

CALLER: *"No that was down by the river. ... It's close to where she is, but that's where I went in the river. ... The policeman's here."*

911 OPERATOR: *"Okay. I'll go ahead and let you go."*

CALLER: *"Okay."*

911 OPERATOR: *"Okay."*

CALLER: *"Thank you very much."*

911 OPERATOR: *"You're welcome."*

CALLER: *"Bye."*

911 OPERATOR: *"Bye bye."(1)*

With that exchange of pleasantries, the call ended. A young mother was dead. But the important thing, at least according to the 911 call, was that her boyfriend was cold.

http://wbp.bz/savingannie1

---

1. *March 16, 2009, Transcript of 911 Call From Stephen P. Nichols to Hood River County Sheriff's Office 911 Call Center*

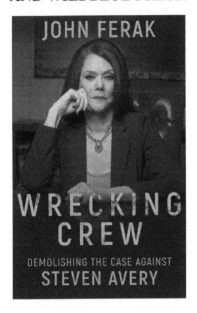
CHAPTER ONE

TURNABOUT

Green Bay's television stations led off their newscasts with a chilling mystery on Thursday night, November 3, 2005. A fiercely independent, happy-go-lucky young woman from the heart of dairy country was gone. No one had seen or heard from her during the past four days. Television anchors painted a grim outlook as photos of Teresa Halbach flashed across the screen. Viewers were left uneasy and fearful of a worst-case scenario. Surely someone watching the distressing news would remember encountering Teresa over the past few days. At least, that's what the small-town Calumet County Sheriff's Office in Chilton, Wisconsin hoped.

But it was not Teresa's face displayed on the television screen that drew a red flag with one of the Manitowoc County residents. It was the image of her missing sports utility vehicle, a Toyota RAV 4.

During that time frame, Kevin Rahmlow lived around Mishicot, a small but proud Wisconsin town of 1,400, people of German, Swiss, and Bohemian heritage. Back in the day, Mishicot had six hotels, three general stores, a movie theater, a grist mill, and a brewery. By 2005, the community's three original churches still stood the test of time but Mishicot looked different. The town's gas station, owned by Cenex, was one of the local hangouts. People came there for fuel, a cup of coffee, and to buy their cigarettes. The popular business was at the corner of State Highway 147 and State Street.

Kevin Rahmlow vividly remembers when he pulled into the Cenex. It was Friday, November 4. Inside the convenience store, the missing person's poster caught his eye. Teresa Marie Halbach, the flier noted, was 5-foot-6, 135 pounds. Brown eyes and light brown hair.

"I remember that the poster had a picture of Teresa Halbach and written descriptions of Teresa Halbach and the car she was driving," Rahmlow said.

As it turned out, Cenex was one of many small-town businesses, bars, and cafes where Teresa's concerned friends and family slapped up posters. They were desperate for answers, hoping somebody, anybody, remembered a sighting. And if the locals didn't see Teresa, perhaps they saw her Toyota RAV4. It had a large Lemieux Toyota sign on the back of her vehicle where the spare tire hung.

When Rahmlow saw the poster, he remembered something.

"On November 3 and 4, 2005, I was in Mishicot. I saw Teresa Halbach's vehicle by the East Twin River dam in Mishicot at the turnabout by the bridge as I drove west of Highway 147. I recognized that the written description of the vehicle on the poster matched the car I saw at the turnaround by the dam."

That Friday afternoon, Rahmlow happened to spot a man in a brown uniform. The man was sporting a badge. "While I was in the Cenex station, a Manitowoc County Sheriff's Department officer came into the station. I immediately told the officer that I had seen a car that matched the description of the car on Teresa Halbach's missing person poster at the turnaround by the dam."

After speaking with the uniformed deputy, Rahmlow went on with his life.

He had no idea whatever became of the matter. He later moved to another Midwest state. He even missed the initial Making a Murderer craze on Netflix that captured world-wide attention.

***

In December 2015, a true crime documentary about the Steven Avery murder case was released on Netflix, but Rahmlow didn't get swept up in the media frenzy. An entire year passed before he finally turned on Netflix to watch it. And as he watched Making a Murderer, the Minnesota man had a flashback. He remembered his encounter at the gas station in Mishicot from more than a decade ago. And besides being familiar with Manitowoc County, Rahmlow knew some of the key people who worked hand in hand with special prosecutor Ken Kratz to cement the guilt of Steven

Avery. Avery, as the world now knows, was a previously wrongfully convicted man who lost eighteen years due to a barbaric daytime rape along the Lake Michigan shoreline during the summer of 1985. This was the crime that allowed dangerous sexual predator Gregory Allen to get away by the forces who ran the Manitowoc County Sheriff's Office, notably Sheriff Tom Kocourek, who was about forty years old at the time.

Fast-forward to 2007. Avery stood trial in Chilton for Teresa's murder even though the prosecution's evidence was like a piece of Swiss cheese. And yet despite his side's many holes, Ken Kratz overcame his murder case's numerous physical evidence shortcomings thanks to the unbelievable eyewitness testimonies from a number of unscrupulous people who very much had a stake, a big stake, in the desired outcome of an Avery guilty verdict.

December 12, 2016

Two weeks before Christmas, Rahmlow sent a text message to someone he recognized from Making a Murderer. By then, Scott Tadych was happily married to Steven Avery's younger sister, Barb. At the time of Teresa's disappearance, Barb Janda lived in one of the trailers at the Avery Salvage Yard compound, a forty-acre tract out in the middle of nowhere surrounded by large gravel pits. At the time of Teresa's disappearance, Barb and Scott Tadych were steady lovers and she was in the process of getting another divorce, this time from Tom Janda.

After watching Making a Murderer, Rahmlow informed his old acquaintance how "I need to get in touch with one of their lawyers."

Rahmlow explained in his text message to Scott Tadych how he recognized Teresa's vehicle as the one he saw by the old dam, either November 3 or 4. He also remembered having a conversation with a man whose face regularly appeared during the Making a Murderer episodes.

Scott Tadych did not respond.

Rahmlow reached out again, ninety minutes later. The second time, he texted his phone number to Tadych. He wanted to discuss the matter over the phone.

"OK, I will I am really sick now can hardly talk so I will call tomorrow," Tadych texted back.

But Tadych never did call back.

"I did not hear from Mr. Tadych the next day or any other day responsive to my request for attorney contact information for Steven Avery or Brendan Dassey," Rahmlow said. "I received another message from Mr. Tadych on December 19 (2016) at 6:10 p.m., which was not responsive to my request."

There is no doubt in his mind that Rahmlow saw Teresa's RAV4 along the rural stretch of two-lane State Highway 147 near the East Twin River Dam. The turnaround on the highway was barely a mile from Avery Salvage.

A licensed private investigator in Illinois and Wisconsin, James R. Kirby was hired by Kathleen T. Zellner & Associates to investigate Teresa's murder case.

"I requested abandoned and towed vehicle reports for the time period of October 31, 2005 through November 5, 2005, from the following agencies: Mishicot Police Department, Two Rivers Police Department, and the Manitowoc County Sheriff's Department," Kirby said.

This, of course, was the period when Teresa was last seen in Manitowoc County, near Mishicot. On a Saturday morning six days later, under highly suspicious circumstances, her Toyota RAV4 turned up, double parked, on the far back ridge of Avery Salvage, near a row of junked vehicles. The spot of the find bordered the massive sand and gravel pit operated by Joshua Radandt.

The question lingered. Who moved Teresa's SUV to the far outer edge of Avery Salvage? Was it the killer working alone? Was it the killer working in tandem with an accomplice? Or was it somebody affiliated with the volunteer search party? Or was it one of the Manitowoc County Sheriff's deputies?

Incidentally, at the time of her disappearance, Teresa's RAV4 had no front-end damage. This small but critical detail is substantiated by the fact that the missing person fliers made no mention of any broken auto parts or wreckage. But when her sports utility vehicle surfaced on the Avery property, it showed heavy front-end damage. Weirdly, the broken blinker light from the driver's side was neatly tucked away into the rear cargo area of the murdered woman's auto. Why would the killer do something so strange? Of course, the logical scenario was that the killer had nothing to do with moving the vehicle to Avery's property, and that the mishap occurred, late at night, during the clandestine efforts to sneak the vehicle onto the Avery property without Avery or his family members catching on.

In any event, private eye Kirby's inquiry into the RAV4 spotted by Rahmlow on Friday afternoon, November 4, 2005, revealed the "Mishicot Police Department had no responsive records. Based upon the response of Two Rivers Police Department and Manitowoc County Sheriff's Office pursuant to my request, none of these agencies logged an abandoned vehicle on Highway 147 near the East Twin River Bridge."

Obviously, one of the most plausible scenarios for why the police did not log the abandoned vehicle spotted near the Old Dam on Highway 147 in rural Manitowoc County, which was Manitowoc County Sheriff's territory, was because the auto belonged to Teresa, and it got moved as a direct result of Manitowoc County's intercession.

CHAPTER TWO

BOBBY DEPARTS

The four Dassey brothers were: Bryan, twenty, Bobby, nineteen, Blaine, almost seventeen, and Brendan, sixteen. As mentioned earlier, the Dasseys occupied one of the mobile home trailers along Avery Road at their family's Avery Salvage Yard compound. Bryan, the oldest brother, worked in nearby Two Rivers at Woodland Face Veneer, a factory overlooking the scenic Lake Michigan.

Regarding the day in question, Oct. 31, 2005, Bryan Dassey told Wisconsin's Division of Criminal Investigation special agents Kim Skorlinski and Debra K. Strauss that he left for his job at 6 a.m. and visited his girlfriend afterward. He was not on Avery Road "except for waking up and going to work. Bryan said he got home sometime after supper but could not recall when that was."

Eventually, the questions steered toward the missing photographer. She had been a regular visitor to the Avery Salvage Yard during the past year without any problems or hassles, unlike at some of her other unnerving Auto Trader assignments where men tried to proposition her or invite her inside their homes for an alcoholic beverage. Whenever Teresa visited Avery Road, she was given courtesy and respect.

"Bryan said he heard from his mom and Steven that Halbach was only at their residence about five minutes. He heard she just took the photo of the van and left. Bryan said the investigators should also talk to his brother Bobby because he saw her leave their property."

At Avery's five-week murder trial in 2007, prosecutor Ken Kratz chose to keep Bryan Dassey off his side's witness stand. Therefore, the jury deciding Steven Avery's fate never heard the following account:

"In October and November 2005, I lived with my girlfriend but I kept my clothing at my mother's trailer, which was on the Avery's Auto Salvage property. On or about (Thursday) November 4, 2005, I returned to my mother's trailer to retrieve some clothes, and I had a conversation with my brother, Bobby, about Teresa Halbach. I distinctly remember Bobby telling me, 'Steven could not have killed her because I saw her leave the property on October 31, 2005."

Bryan Dassey's October 2017 sworn affidavit recalled how he was pulled over by police on November 6, 2005. He was behind the wheel of his uncle Steven Avery's Pontiac.

"My brother Brendan was in the car with me, and he was interviewed by other officers at the same time as me. I told the investigators that they should talk to my brother Bobby because he saw Teresa Halbach leave the Avery property on October 31, 2005.

"I was not called as a witness to testify at my Uncle Steven's criminal trial."

***

Most of the world who watched Making a Murderer fell in love with Steven Avery's private counsel, Dean Strang and Jerome Buting. The two criminal defense lawyers worked closely together, putting forth a heroic defense for their client at his murder trial, but even they now admit that, in retrospect, they overlooked some things along the way.

They had hired Conrad "Pete" Baetz, a retired police detective, as their investigator in preparation for trial. Baetz had moved back to his native Manitowoc County after his retirement in downstate Illinois. He had spent many years at the Madison County Sheriff's Office near St. Louis.

"I have reviewed the police report of the November 6, 2005, interview of Bryan Dassey where he said that Bobby Dassey saw Teresa Halbach leave the Avery property on October 31, 2005. I was unaware of this report. I never tried to interview Bryan Dassey about Bobby Dassey's alleged statement. I was never instructed by trial defense counsel Buting and Strang to interview Bryan Dassey," Baetz said.

"Bobby Dassey was the key prosecution witness at Steven Avery's trial who testified that he saw Ms. Halbach walk towards Mr. Avery's trailer after taking photographs of his mother Barb Janda's van. Bobby also testified that when he left the Avery Salvage Yard, Ms. Halbach's vehicle was still on the property."

In hindsight, Baetz realized that the statement had major significance.

"If the trial defense counsel could have impeached Bobby Dassey with Bryan Dassey's testimony that Bobby admitted he saw Ms. Halbach leave the Avery Salvage Yard, it would have undermined the State's entire case against Mr. Avery, and there would have been a reasonable probability of him being found not guilty."

http://wbp.bz/wca

More True Crime You'll Love From WildBlue Press

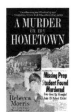

A MURDER IN MY HOMETOWN by Rebecca Morris
Nearly 50 years after the murder of seventeen year old Dick Kitchel, Rebecca Morris returned to her hometown to write about how the murder changed a town, a school, and the lives of his friends.

wbp.bz/hometowna

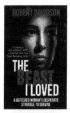

THE BEAST I LOVED by Robert Davidson
Robert Davidson again demonstrates that he is a master of psychological horror in this riveting and hypnotic story ... I was so enthralled that I finished the book in a single sitting. "—James Byron Huggins, International Bestselling Author of The Reckoning

wbp.bz/tbila

BULLIED TO DEATH by Judith A. Yates
On September 5, 2015, in a public park in LaVergne, Tennessee, fourteen-year-old Sherokee Harriman drove a kitchen knife into her stomach as other teens watched in horror. Despite attempts to save her, the girl died, and the coroner ruled it a "suicide." But was it? Or was it a crime perpetuated by other teens who had bullied her?

wbp.bz/btda

SUMMARY EXECUTION by Michael Withey
"An incredible true story that reads like an international crime thriller peopled with assassins, political activists, shady FBI informants, murdered witnesses, a tenacious attorney, and a murderous foreign dictator. "—Steve Jackson, New York Times bestselling author of NO STONE UNTURNED

wbp.bz/sea

Manufactured by Amazon.ca
Bolton, ON

18036371R00125